I GOT A DIVORCE

A Christian's Guide to Surviving Divorce, Recovering Your Heart, and Discovering New Beginnings

By:

Teresa McKelvey

Copyright Page

I Got A Divorce: A Christian's Guide to Surviving Divorce, Recovering Your Heart, and Discovering New Beginnings

Published by
Whispering Pines Publishing House
733 Freeman Road
Dadeville, AL 36853

First Edition

ISBN: 979-8-9945144-0-5

Cover design by JMedia

Important Note:

This book is based on personal experience and is intended to offer hope, encouragement, and practical guidance during a difficult season. It is not a substitute for professional counseling, therapy, or medical advice. If you are experiencing severe emotional distress, depression, or thoughts of self-harm, please seek help from a qualified mental health professional immediately.

The stories and experiences shared in this book come from real life, but some details have been changed to protect privacy.

Connect with Teresa:

Website: teresamckelvey.com
YouTube: Tea Time with Teresa

Printed in the United States of America

Dedication Page

This book exists because Gaye Hagan refused to let me stay stuck in my own fear and self-doubt. She helped me understand that my biggest failure could become my greatest ministry, that my deepest pain could become someone else's healing.

Gaye, your constant support, your unwavering belief, and your gentle pushing when I needed it most made this possible.

Thank you for seeing what God was doing even when I couldn't. Thank you for not letting me waste the calling He placed on my life. And thank you for teaching me that sometimes the very thing we want to run from is exactly what the world needs us to walk toward.

With deepest gratitude,

Teresa

Thank You

To those who helped edit, proof read, and scripturally look over the book. I am so very thankful for your help, advice, and mostly prayers. Thank you for helping this book come to life.

Table of Contents

Introduction: **You Are Not Alone**

I tried to run from this book. I tried to write anything and everything else. I argued with God, "Lord please just let me entertain your people, let me create fun videos on YouTube, let me interview others and tell their stories. Anything God, but that. Anything but my divorce, my pain, my shame." God, why does it have to be me? I spent more than a year trying to convince God to give up this call for me to write this book. Alas, He made it very clear nothing else I could try and do was going to succeed if I didn't write this book. To say I have been like Jonah in the whale is probably an understatement. I have wallowed in self-pity and tried my best to convince God of so many other things I could do for Him other than this book. At night I would cry out to Him, "Why does my platform have to be my biggest failure?" God kept saying write the book. Dear reader, I tell you all of this so that when I say God wanted you to know the words of this book, you will believe me.

I remember sitting in my car outside the bookstore, working up the courage to go inside and look for something, anything, that would speak to my reality. I was thinking, "There's not going to be one. There's just going to be a hundred books on how to heal your marriage, and there's not going to be a devotional about me, my trauma, my reality." I felt so alone, like I was the only Christian who had ever walked this road.

Years later, when Jeff and I met and eventually married, we discovered we had both traveled this same painful path. He had his own story of feeling isolated from his church community, not knowing who to talk to or where to go for support that understood both his faith and his circumstances. We both had searched for resources that spoke directly to Christians going through divorce, and we both came up short.

That's when we knew – God had brought us together not just for our own healing, but to create what we couldn't find when we needed it most. We spent hours talking through our individual experiences, comparing what worked, what didn't work, and what we desperately wished someone had told us during those darkest days.

Jeff is not a writer but his fingerprints are all over this work. His quiet wisdom, his different perspective, and his own journey through survival, recovery, and thriving have shaped every chapter of this book. We've laughed together, cried together, and prayed together over every word, wanting to make sure we're giving you exactly what we needed when we were in your shoes.

This isn't just my story or his story – it's our story, crafted specifically for you because we remember what it felt like to feel so alone in our pain. We want you to know from the very first page: you are not alone. We've been where you are, we understand your pain, and more importantly than us knowing your pain – God knows your pain and He is with you.

Whatever has brought you to this book, whether you were left or the one to leave, whether it was a sudden ending or a gradual building up, however you find yourself in this situation, I want you to know that not only do I feel your pain and I completely understand your struggle, but even more importantly so does God. Not many Christians will tell you this when you mention divorce and yet this is exactly what God has called me to tell you in this book. God is with you. He sees you. He is in the middle of this new reality that seems so far removed from anything God would have anything to do with. That's because God is with us in our hurts, our pain, our loss, our brokenness. If all you read of this book is this page, then let me tell you everything I learned going through this situation: God is with you. Please don't just read over that – God is with you. He loves you and He has made me miserable because I kept trying not to write this book and He wanted you to get this message. This book is God's gift to you. Please take this book, pour over the pages and start right off by asking God what He wants to say to you. Read it slowly, absorb the words God is impressing on my heart to write to you. God is in the middle of your situation. Trust me, He was with me and I grew closer to Him because of this absolutely painful experience and so can you.

It is a new reality that you must accept but that doesn't happen overnight. Truth is it will come in waves and it will come as you grow closer to God.

I hope this book will help you process your new reality and bring you some relief in one of the most painful things we can experience. I will also let you in on a secret – there is nothing in this book that is an Einstein moment. I am going to tell you the basic truths and some of the most simple ideas and practices that you already know. However, when you are in the midst of accepting a new reality, no matter what that new reality may be, sometimes we forget the most basic life-giving practices. This book is a guide to show you the way to maneuver in your new reality and make it as less painful as possible.

Please know that you are not alone. I have been where you are and I have felt this pain and had my own experience accepting my new reality. More importantly than me knowing your pain, God knows your pain and He is with you.

This book isn't a guide about if you should or should not divorce. This isn't a guide on how to carry out a divorce. This book is a guide for those going through the trauma of divorce.

When you are in the middle of a traumatic life event, everything in your life is shaken at the very foundation of who you are. I found that during a trauma the most helpful thing is to simplify everything and find someone to walk it through with you. Having a friend come alongside you to tell you they are with you, they understand your pain, and they are able to offer tips that helped them through the same situation is invaluable.

During my divorce I didn't have that. I had many well-meaning people support me during that time but no one who really got what I was going through and could offer suggestions based on proven results. So I searched for a book. I searched for programs and resources. There was nothing that I could find that appealed to me. I didn't want to read or hear about someone else's drama, I was caught up in my own. I didn't want anyone to preach at me how I was supposed to feel and think. Watching movies of how others had handled divorce was a complete train wreck. *Under the Tuscan Sun*... bad idea.

Once I felt emotionally and mentally at peace from my divorce, I went back and read over my journals and sat down and wrote out what worked for me and what didn't work for me. In doing that I came to realize these were common sense things that honestly helped me and made a huge difference for me. I could see that the things I stumbled on allowed me to process my divorce period a little faster and easier than others around me who I could tell were still in the trauma of their divorce.

I also was able to clearly see that there are three different stages of what I call a divorce period. And each of those stages require different techniques in order to manage the stage in the best way.

In this book I outline the three stages and I offer techniques that I believe will complement and help you achieve each stage.

This is not a step-by-step guide on how to do something kind of book, because we are not one-size-fits-all humans. We are unique in our design so some techniques may work better for you while others don't. This book is simply a guide along that journey that no one wants to go on and yet a large percentage of us humans find ourselves there. This book can be used for men or women, yourself or someone you know is going through a divorce, and though I am a Christian and do offer some techniques that apply to Christians, this book can be used for unbelievers as well.

I discovered through my analyzing of my own divorce period and others around me that there are really three significant periods you will go through.

In this book you will find the three parts or stages. The stages do not have a set time period and you can switch back and forth between the first two. The last stage is only accomplished once the first two have truly been completed and that is up to the person walking through that stage.

I recommend you read the whole book, then find the stage you believe you are in and read through that stage slowly, asking yourself what works for you and what doesn't. What works, make it a habit and stick to it. Do it until you no longer need to do it and then move on to the next stage.

Survival is the first step because if you don't survive this stage the other stages are worthless. This is like going to the ER. After the trauma has subsided and you are in a stable place you move to **Recovery**, and once you are fully recovered and been through therapy you can then move on to **Thriving**. These stages will most likely be months and years apart from each other.

Please understand my heart. I didn't write this book because I did everything right and sailed through my divorce with no trauma or massive mistakes. The opposite is true and that is exactly why I felt led to write this book. I am no expert in anything. What this book is based on is my real world experience along with conversation and research of others who have also gone through this experience. My prayer is that this book will help at least one person through their divorce with a little less pain and a faster transition to thriving in their life again.

Before we continue, Jeff and I want to remind you that we are not licensed professionals, counselors, or medical experts. We're just two people who found ourselves as Christians going through divorce and felt alone during that journey. What we're sharing are simple tips and practices that helped us in our recovery, not professional medical or therapeutic advice. If you need professional help, please seek out qualified counselors, therapists, or medical professionals.

Part One: Survival

Chapter 1: The Pain

Giving yourself permission to hurt with boundaries

"The Lord is close to the brokenhearted and saves those who are crushed in spirit." - Psalm 34:18

When Jeff and I were putting this journey together, we were discussing the things that we really went through and what would have helped us had we known, if someone had told us. That is how this whole book came about. We also really thought that when you're hurting, when you are in drama, when you are in trauma, you need triage. You need someone to come along and tell you "Here, drink this, here do this" because your body is in shock, your emotions are in shock, and you do not know the basic things you need to do in order to take care of yourself.

That is what this chapter is supposed to be - it is supposed to come alongside you as the body of Christ to tell you that you are not alone and "here, drink this, lean on me, I'll help you through this."

Today it is all about letting yourself hurt. And I am calling it that because there are two things with this that are important. One, is we believe that you need to give yourself permission to hurt. And two, the reason a lot of people don't want to give themselves permission to hurt is because they're afraid they will become consumed by it. So we'd like to offer you a sort of tool for that, and that is to find a space and to get a timer, put a timer on allowing yourself to absolutely feel your emotions.

Let me tell you something that might surprise you - one of the biggest mistakes I see people make during divorce recovery is trying not to feel the pain. I get it. The pain is overwhelming. It's scary. It feels like if you really let yourself feel it, you might never stop crying, you might never get out of bed, you might just completely fall apart and never be able to put yourself back together.

But here's what I learned the hard way - that pain you're trying not to feel? It doesn't go away just because you ignore it. It sits there in your chest, in your stomach, in your shoulders. It shows up as anger at inappropriate times. It shows up as anxiety about things that never used to bother you. It shows up as numbness when you should be feeling joy.

The pain has to go somewhere. And if you don't give it a proper place to land, it's going to land everywhere, all over your life, all over the people you love.

When I was going through my divorce, I tried so hard to be strong. I tried to be the person everyone could count on. I went to work every day, I took care of my responsibilities, I smiled when people asked how I was doing. And inside, I was dying. I was absolutely dying, and I thought that was what being strong looked like.

One day I was in the shower - you know how the shower is sometimes the only place where you can really let your guard down - and I just started sobbing. I mean ugly crying, the kind where you can't catch your breath, where your whole body is shaking. And I realized I hadn't really cried, really let myself feel the enormity of what I was losing, since the day I knew for sure my marriage was over. I had been so busy being strong that I hadn't given myself permission to be human.

Here's something they don't teach you in church but that I wish someone had told me - hurting is not just an emotion, it's a physical process. What I experienced was that when you lose something significant, your body goes through an actual physiological response. I

read that your brain has to literally rewire itself to accommodate this new reality where this person, this future, this life you planned is no longer there.

That takes energy. It takes time. And it takes feeling. You know how when you break a bone, you don't just ignore it and expect it to heal properly? You have to set it, you have to rest it, you have to go through the process of healing. I personally believe emotional trauma works the same way. You can't just ignore a broken heart and expect it to heal properly.

The pain you're feeling isn't a sign that something is wrong with you. The pain you're feeling is a sign that something was right with you - that you loved deeply, that you invested fully, that you gave your whole heart to something that mattered to you. The depth of your pain is a testament to the depth of your love.

Don't be ashamed of that pain. Honor it.

Now, having said all that, I also need to tell you that pain without boundaries can destroy you. I've seen people get stuck in their pain, get stuck in their anger, get stuck in their hurt to the point where it becomes their identity. Years later, they're still talking about their divorce like it happened yesterday. They're still consumed by bitterness, still defined by what was done to them.

That's not healing in my opinion. That's not honoring your pain. That's making your pain your god. So we need to give our pain a place, but we also need to give it limits.

A lot of women go to the bathroom when they need to cry, and I think it's two-fold. One reason is because sometimes that's the only place you can get away from children or from others who live in your home. But also it's a place where you are confronted with the mirror - you can go all day long and not really deal with your emotions, but all of a sudden you see yourself in that mirror and it reflects you back to you. You see the pain in your eyes and on your face and you see the hurt, and you're confronted with it and you don't have a choice but to deal with it.

For men, that might be different. It might be taking a drive somewhere, or going for a walk, or going to the garage and pretending like you're working on something. We all have a space where we can let our guard down and feel what we feel.

You should during this time, have a space, a place where you can go and let it all down and feel what you feel. But you also need guardrails around that. You need to be able to say, "Okay, from my drive from here to here, I'm going to feel and just deal with this. But when I get there, I'm going to shut it down."

That gives you permission to feel it, that gives you some sort of control over it, to realize that "okay, I can let these emotions be what they are, but then I'm going to put them back in their box until the next time." These two things are really important; to give yourself permission to feel what you feel, and then putting some guardrails on it. Guardrails are space and time.

You might have no children and be going through this in a home where you could just feel what you feel all the time, you don't have to worry about it impacting others. However a lot of people that I know who go through divorce, you have other people that it's impacting and you can't impact them with your feelings, with your emotions. Sometimes you've got to be the strong person that they're leaning on.

But that doesn't mean that you don't hurt. That doesn't mean that you just don't deal with your feelings. Matter of fact, I think you have more responsibility to deal with those feelings, to model how to deal with intense emotions, and that's by having a space and a time restriction on it.

Let me give you some practical examples of what this might look like:

Time boundaries:

- "I'm going to let myself cry for 20 minutes, and then I'm going to wash my face and go make dinner."

Space boundaries:

- "The bathroom is where I go to cry."
- "I can be a mess in my bedroom, but when I come downstairs, I'm present for my kids."
- "My car is my safe space to scream or sob or just sit in the silence."

I want to be really clear about something - giving yourself permission to hurt doesn't mean wallowing. It doesn't mean staying in your pajamas for three weeks straight. It doesn't mean neglecting your responsibilities or your children or your health. Healthy hurting looks like honoring your pain without being controlled by it.

Some days, healthy hurting might look like crying in the shower for ten minutes and then getting dressed and going to work. Some days it might look like canceling plans because you just don't have it in you, and that's okay too. Some days it might look like forcing yourself to go out with friends even though you don't feel like it, because you know isolation isn't good for you.

The key is being intentional about it. Not just letting your emotions drive the bus, but also not trying to stuff them in the trunk and pretend they're not there.

Jeff and I deal with emotional pain very differently. When I'm processing something difficult, I need to talk it out. I need to cry it out. I need to journal it out. I'm very external in my processing. Jeff is the opposite. When he's processing something difficult, he gets quiet. He goes internal. He might go work on a project in the garage where he can think. He might go for a long hike. He needs space and silence to process.

Neither of these is right or wrong - they're just different. The important thing is knowing how you process your emotions and giving yourself what you need in order to do that.

If you're an external processor like me, you might need:

- A friend who will just listen without trying to fix you
- A journal to write out all your thoughts and feelings
- A therapist or counselor to help you work through things
- Time to cry out loud, to scream if you need to

If you're an internal processor, you might need:

- Alone time without anyone asking how you're doing
- Physical activities that let your mind wander
- Creative outlets like art or music or building something
- Space to think without having to explain yourself to anyone

Sometimes hurting gets complicated. Sometimes the pain becomes so overwhelming that you can't function. Sometimes the boundaries you've set aren't enough to contain it. Sometimes you find yourself having thoughts that scare you.

If that happens, please, please get help. There's no shame in needing more support than a friend or a book can provide. There's no shame in needing medication or therapy or intensive counseling. I'm not a therapist, I'm just someone who's been through this. And part of being someone who's been through this is knowing when to say "I need more help than I can give myself."

Some signs that you might need professional help:

- You can't sleep for more than a few hours at a time for weeks on end
- You can't eat or you can't stop eating
- You're having thoughts of hurting yourself
- You can't function at work or take care of your children
- You're using alcohol or drugs to numb the pain
- It's been months and you're not seeing any improvement in your ability to cope

There's no shame in any of this. Divorce is one of the most stressful life events a person can go through. Getting help isn't a sign of weakness - it's a sign of wisdom.

I want to tell you something that might be hard to hear right now, but that I think is important. Your pain has a purpose. I'm not saying that everything happens for a reason - I hate that phrase and I think it's cruel to say to someone who's hurting. But I am saying that your pain can have a purpose if you let it.

Your pain can teach you things about yourself that you never would have learned otherwise. It can show you how strong you really are. It can deepen your compassion for others who are suffering. It can strip away things that don't really matter and help you see what does.

Your pain can be a teacher, but only if you're willing to feel it and learn from it instead of just trying to make it go away as fast as possible. My friend, I need you to know something. This pain you're feeling right now? It won't last forever. I know it feels like it will. I know it feels like you'll never be happy again, like you'll never feel normal again, like this ache in your chest will be there for the rest of your life. But it won't.

The pain will change. It will become less sharp, less constant, less consuming. It will become something you carry instead of something that carries you. It will become a scar instead of an open wound. And you know what? That scar will remind you of your own strength. It will remind you of your capacity to love deeply and to survive loss. It will remind you that you are more resilient than you ever imagined.

But first, you have to feel it. You have to honor it. You have to give it the space and time it needs to do its work in you.

Scripture for Comfort:

"Weeping may stay for the night, but rejoicing comes in the morning."
- Psalm 30:5

"He heals the brokenhearted and binds up their wounds." - Psalm 147:3

Chapter 2: You NEED a Hiding Place

"You are my hiding place; you will protect me from trouble and surround me with songs of deliverance." - Psalm 32:7

When you realize you're going through a divorce as a Christian, you immediately feel alienated. From your family, from your friends, but especially from God, from your faith, from your church. I'm here to tell you that the body of Christ is still here with you in this, and God is in this with you too. You are not alone!

Let me tell you what happened to me. When I realized and accepted that I was getting a divorce, I got in my car and drove over to my local bookstore. I think mine was Books-A-Million. The whole way over there, I was like, "I need a devotional. I just need a Christian devotional." And there's not going to be one. There's just going to be "how to heal your marriage" and "how to do this" and "how to do that," and there's not going to be a devotional about me, about my trauma, about my reality.

So I go in there, I go down the aisle, and I look. I'm looking for the words "divorce" and "Christian" - I just want to see those two words together, you know, not in a condemnation way, but in a helpful way. And I look, and there it is. I was in shock.

The book was called *Divorce Care: Hope, Help and Healing During and After Your Divorce* - 365 daily devotions by Steve Grissom and Kathy Leonard. I bought that book, I bought a pen, and I treated that book as a journal. I mean, I wrote on every single page. I would read it, I would absorb it, and then I even did more than one a day. I just absorbed that book.

Years later, I did more research and found out that there's even a small group program that churches can have, which I highly, recommend. There's a whole recovery program by DivorceCare - not just a book, they have videos and you can meet in groups and do a workbook together.

Here's what I want you to understand: finding that book was like finding water in the desert. It told me I wasn't crazy, I wasn't alone, and I wasn't the first Christian to walk through divorce. Sometimes that's all we need - just to know we're not the only one.

Jeff and I pulled together these resources we offer in this book because what led to full recovery and healing was more than a daily devotional reading for us and we wanted to offer those same resources to you.

Now, I want to talk about the second resource I discovered, and this one is so important. This is a time when you might feel that God has forsaken you, that God is not with you in this situation. You might think it can't be, because "God hates divorce," right? We're going to address that verse later in this book, but right now I want you to know something: God doesn't forsake us. God is with us in our pain, in every situation. He's with us.

At the time, I had a King James Version Bible, and I just couldn't... all those "thees" and "thous" I just couldn't in that emotional state comprehend it in a way that I needed to. So I went and found an easier version of the Bible for me to understand. Then I just started reading Genesis. I was like, "I'm just going to start with the first one," and I went through the whole Bible. I went through it so quickly, and part of it was because I was reading an easier version for me to absorb.

But really, I just dove deep into the Bible. I put my attention on knowing who God is. You know that verse where David says, "You are my hiding place"? This is what called out to me and became my truth. I needed a hiding place and God was offering me one and you, my friend need that. You are in such deep pain, you're in a place where you just need to hide in the Word of God, and you can. This is your time to do it. Take this resource - your Bible - and just hide in there. Just go in there, dive deep into it.

Don't try to understand it or seek to learn something new - just read it. Just every day, go in and read the Bible. You can start from Revelation and go backward if you want. I just started with Genesis 1:1. I was just reading. I didn't know what God was going to tell me. I wasn't even reading it with a purpose. I was just hiding. God was my hiding place, and I just hid in His Word and you can too.

Here's what I learned about hiding places: you have to be intentional about creating them. When you're going through divorce, everything feels unsafe. Your home might not feel safe because of the memories. Your church might not feel safe because of the questions. Your friend group might not feel safe because people don't know what to say.

But God's Word? That's always safe. That's always available. That's always true, no matter what your circumstances look like.

I had to learn to self-protect during this time. I'm not talking about building walls or shutting people out completely - I'm talking about being wise about what you expose your wounded heart to. You know how when you have a physical wound, you keep it clean and covered while it heals? Your heart needs the same kind of protection.

The Bible became my bandage. When thoughts would race through my mind - thoughts about the future, about what people were saying, about whether I'd made the right decisions - I would open that book and read until my mind settled. Sometimes it was just one verse. Sometimes it was a whole chapter. But I always found what I needed in those pages.

Let me be practical with you for a minute. If you're struggling to understand the version of the Bible you have, get a different one. There's no shame in that. The New Living Translation, the NIV - find one that speaks to your heart in this season. The goal isn't to impress anyone with what version you're reading. The goal is to meet with God.

I remember reading Psalm 34:18 in my new, easier-to-understand Bible: **"The Lord is close to the brokenhearted and saves those who are crushed in spirit." In the King James, that same verse reads: "The Lord is nigh unto them that are of a broken heart;**

and saveth such as be of a contrite spirit." Both are true, but in that season, I needed the first one. I needed to hear that God was "close," not "nigh." I needed words that felt like a friend talking to me, not like a textbook.

Your heart is broken right now. You don't need fancy language - you need truth that penetrates right to where you hurt.

Here's something nobody tells you about reading the Bible during trauma: it becomes a discipline that actually heals you in ways you don't expect. When I first started reading every day, it was purely survival. I was drowning, and God's Word was my life preserver. But as days turned into weeks, something shifted.

I started looking forward to that time. Not because the pain was gone - it wasn't. But because for thirty minutes or an hour each day, I was focused on something bigger than my circumstances. I was reminded of who God is, even when I couldn't figure out who I was anymore.

Some days I would read about God's faithfulness and think, "Where is that faithfulness in my life?" Other days I would read about His love and feel it wash over me like a warm blanket. Both responses were okay. God can handle our questions, our anger, our confusion. He's not intimidated by our pain.

The beautiful thing about hiding in God's Word during this season is that you're not trying to become a Bible scholar or win any spiritual maturity awards. You're just surviving. And God honors that. He meets us where we are, not where we think we should be.

Your Survival Kit

So here's what I want you to walk away with from this second chapter. Think of these as the contents of your survival kit - the things you absolutely need to get through the hardest days:

1. **A version of the Bible you can understand** - Don't worry about what anyone else thinks. Get one that speaks to your heart.
2. **A daily routine of reading** - Even if it's just five minutes. Even if you don't feel like it. Even if you don't understand what you're reading. Just show up.
3. **A journal or some way to write** - Whether it's in the margins of that DivorceCare book like I did, or a separate notebook, give yourself a place to process what you're reading and feeling.
4. **Permission to hide** - You don't have to be strong for everyone right now. It's okay to pull back, to say no to things, to protect your heart while it heals.

Remember, this is triage. We're just trying to stop the bleeding right now. We're not trying to run a marathon or climb a mountain. We're just trying to make it through today, and then tomorrow, and then the next day.

God is your hiding place. His Word is your safe space. And slowly, day by day, as you hide in Him, you'll find that you're not just surviving - you're actually beginning to heal.

You're going to make it through this. I promise you that. Not because I have some special insight, but because I've seen God's faithfulness in my own story and in the stories of so many others. You're not alone, and you never will be.

Scripture to Memorize:

"The Lord is close to the brokenhearted and saves those who are crushed in spirit." - Psalm 34:18

Chapter 3: Be Toxic

When you need to be that friend who just needs to vent

"Carry each other's burdens, and in this way you will fulfill the law of Christ." - Galatians 6:2

This is one time, my friend, in life when you are really allowed to be that toxic friend. Whether you have friends, family members, a club you belong to, or just co-workers - this is your time to just be toxic.

I know that sounds terrible. I know we live in a world where everyone's talking about cutting toxic people out of your life, avoiding toxic relationships, staying away from toxic situations. But you know what? This is your time to acknowledge your hurt, your pain, and find people who you can be toxic around. Call it being toxic, be selfish, speak, feel, cry, do what you need to do to feel better.

There's a scene in the movie Sleepless in Seattle where Tom Hanks's wife has died and a friend comes over, well-meaning, and gives him a therapist or counselor's card. The Character Tom portrays is fed up and he pulls open his drawer and starts tossing all the well meaning cards his friends, co-workers and family have given him. Finally he says, "Don't mind me, I'm just a guy who's lost his wife." And that's exactly it - this is your time to be toxic. Don't worry about your response being correct, just be honest.

Now let me be clear about what I mean when I say "be toxic," because I'm not talking about being cruel or abusive or destructive. I'm not talking about lashing out at innocent people or treating others terribly because you're hurting.

What I'm talking about is being that friend who needs more than they can give right now. Being that person who's all about themselves for a season. Being honest about the fact that you don't have the emotional bandwidth to be anyone's cheerleader, problem-solver, or shoulder to cry on because you're drowning in your own stuff.

I'm talking about giving yourself permission to be needy. To be the one who calls crying. To be the one who needs to talk for two hours straight without reciprocating. To be the one who can't handle anyone else's problems right now because your own problems are taking up all your available mental and emotional space.

In our culture, especially in Christian culture, we're taught to be selfless. We're taught to put others first, to be the helper, to be strong for everyone else. And those are good things - in normal circumstances. But these are not normal circumstances. This is crisis mode. This is triage. And in triage, the most important thing is stopping the bleeding and we can do that by being toxic with others.

When you're going through a divorce, you are in survival mode. Your entire world has been turned upside down. Your future has been erased. Your identity has been shattered. Your daily routine, your living situation, your financial security, your children's stability - everything is up in the air.

This is not the time to worry about being a balanced friend who gives as much as they take. This is not the time to worry about being the strong one for everyone else. This is not the time to pretend you're fine when you're falling apart.

You know what happens when you try to be strong for everyone else while you're drowning? You go under. And then you're no good to anyone, including yourself. I learned this the hard way. During my divorce, I was still trying to be the friend everyone could count on. When someone called with their problems, I listened. When someone needed help, I said yes. When someone asked how I was doing, I said "fine" and immediately turned the conversation back to them.

I thought I was being a good friend. I thought I was being strong. What I was actually doing was denying myself the support I desperately needed while pouring from an empty cup. One day, I was on the phone with a friend who was telling me about some drama in her marriage - nothing serious, just typical relationship stuff. And I found myself getting so angry. Not at her, but at the situation. Here I was, my entire life falling apart, and I'm listening to someone complain about her husband leaving dishes in the sink.

That's when I realized I needed to have some honest conversations with the people in my life.

How to Be A "Toxic Teresa / Toxic Jeff"

So how do you be toxic without actually being toxic? How do you be honest about your needs without being a terrible person?

Be upfront about where you are. Instead of pretending you're fine, tell people the truth. "Hey, I need you to know that I'm going through a really hard time right now and I'm not going to be a very good friend for a while. I need more than I can give, and I need you to be okay with that."

Ask for what you need. "Can I just vent to you right now? Can I be toxic in this relationship for a little bit, please?" You'd be surprised how many people will say yes when you're honest about what you need.

Set boundaries around what you can handle. "I love you and I want to support you, but I can't handle hearing about relationship problems right now. Can we table that for a few months?" or "I'm not in a place where I can give advice right now, but I can listen if you just need someone to hear you."

Be specific about the kind of support you need. "I don't need you to fix this or give me advice. I just need you to listen and tell me I'm not crazy." or "I need you to let me cry and not try to cheer me up." or "I need you to sit with me in this mess and not try to clean it up."

Not everyone can handle your toxic season, and that's okay. Some people are fair-weather friends - they're great when life is good, but they disappear when things get messy. Some people are fixers who can't handle problems they can't solve. Some people are so uncomfortable with pain that they'll do anything to make it stop, even if that means dismissing your feelings.

You need to find your safe people - the ones who can sit with you in your mess without trying to clean it up. The ones who can listen to you say the same thing for the hundredth time without getting frustrated. The ones who won't judge you for falling apart or try to rush you through your grief.

These people might surprise you. Sometimes the people you think will be there for you aren't, and sometimes people you barely know show up in the most amazing ways.

My safe people during my divorce were:

- My sister, who brought me a "happy divorce scarf" and let me cry on her shoulder whenever I needed to
- A friend from work who had been through her own divorce and could listen without trying to fix me
- My pastor, who surprised me by saying "sometimes divorce is the least bad option" when I expected judgment
- A neighbor I barely knew who saw me crying in my driveway and brought me a casserole and a hug

There's something very therapeutic about hearing yourself say something that you're thinking and feeling. Sometimes we can say things and the moment you hear it, it is a realization. Once it's out, you might realize "oh, I'm done with that" or "you know what, I don't really think that. I think I just felt it. I didn't really think it, I just felt it." Or "I didn't know that wasn't really something that's written on the tablet of my heart, it's just something right now I'm thinking and feeling."

We really need to voice it. We need to be toxic during this time. You need to give yourself permission to not be at all times everyone's go-to person, and give people the ability to help you. They want to help you, they want to support you, but you have to give them permission.

By saying "hey, can I be toxic right now? Can I just be your toxic friend for a little while?" you're actually giving them a gift. You're giving them the opportunity to show up for you in your time of need. You're giving them a chance to be the friend to you that they would want someone to be to them if they were in your shoes.

What "Being Toxic" Might Look Like Practically

Let me give you some real examples of what this might look like in your life:

Calling someone and saying: "I need to talk for thirty minutes about how angry I am, and I need you to just listen and agree with me that this sucks. I don't need advice, I don't need perspective, I just need to be mad out loud."

Texting someone: "I'm having a really bad day and I need to complain about everything for a while. Are you free to be my complaint department?"

Telling your family: "I know I'm not fun to be around right now. I know I'm negative and sad and self-absorbed. I'm working on it, but this is where I am for now, and I need you to be patient with me."

Being honest with your friends: "I can't handle hearing about your problems right now. It's not that I don't care about you, it's that I literally don't have the emotional capacity to take on anything else."

Asking for specific help: "Can you come sit with me while I cry?" or "Can you help me box up his stuff because I can't do it alone?" or "Can you come grocery shopping with me because normal tasks feel overwhelming right now?"

Now, I need to be clear about something - being toxic can't be a permanent way of life. At some point, you need to start giving back to the people who supported you through your darkest time. At some point, you need to start being the friend who can handle other people's problems again. But that's not today. And it might not be for a while, and that's okay.

When I was in my toxic season, I told my closest friends, "I need about six months where I'm going to be a terrible friend. I'm going to need more than I can give, and I'm going to be self-absorbed and needy. After that, I promise I'll start working on being a better friend again, but right now I just need you to carry me."

Most of them said yes. The ones who couldn't handle it, well, I learned something important about those relationships.

The Difference Between Being Toxic and Being Abusive

I want to be really clear about the difference between being toxic in a healthy way and being actually toxic or abusive. Being toxic in a healthy way means:

- Being honest about your needs and limitations
- Asking for more support than you can give right now
- Setting boundaries around what you can handle
- Being self-absorbed for a season while you heal
- Needing to vent and process out loud

Being actually toxic or abusive means:

- Taking your pain out on innocent people
- Being cruel or deliberately hurtful
- Refusing to take any responsibility for your behavior
- Making everything about you all the time, even after you're no longer in crisis
- Using your pain as an excuse to treat people badly

The key difference is intention and awareness. When you're being toxic in a healthy way, you're aware that you're asking for more than you can give, you're grateful for the support, and you have every intention of reciprocating when you're able. When you're being actually toxic, you feel entitled to treat people however you want because you're hurting, and you have no intention of changing or improving.

Maybe you're reading this and thinking, "That sounds great, but I don't have anyone I can be toxic with. I don't have anyone who can handle my mess." First, I'm sorry. That's really hard, and it makes an already difficult situation even more isolating.

Grab a journal and be toxic on paper. I'm not talking about pretty journaling with thoughtful reflections and neat handwriting. I'm talking about messy, angry, stream-of-consciousness writing where you just dump everything you're thinking and feeling onto the page.

Write about how unfair this is. Write about how angry you are. Write about your fears, your resentments, your disappointments. Write about how much you hate having to start over. Write it all out, and don't worry about it making sense or being appropriate or being "Christian enough."

This isn't journaling for posterity - this is journaling for survival. You might burn these pages later, or delete the document, or throw the notebook away. That's fine. The point isn't to keep it forever; the point is to get it out of your head and heart so it stops poisoning you from the inside.

Sometimes we need to hear ourselves say things out loud, and sometimes we need to see our thoughts on paper to realize what we're really feeling versus what we just think we're feeling.

When journaling isn't enough here are some other options:

Find a therapist or counselor. They are literally paid to listen to your problems without judgment. They can handle your toxic season because it's their job and they're trained for it.

Look for support groups. DivorceCare groups, church support groups, online forums - places where everyone is going through something similar and understands the need to be self-focused for a while.

Reach out to acquaintances who've been through divorce. You'd be surprised how willing people are to help when you're honest about what you need. That coworker who got divorced last year? That neighbor whose husband left? They remember what it felt like, and they might be more willing to listen than you think.

Consider online counseling or support. If you can't find local support, there are online options where you can connect with people who understand what you're going through.

I want you to understand something - when you let people support you during your toxic season, you're not just taking from them. You're giving them something too. You're giving them the gift of being needed. You're giving them the opportunity to make a real difference in someone's life. You're giving them a chance to show love in action, not just in words.

Most people want to help when someone they care about is struggling. They just don't know how. By being specific about what you need, by giving them permission to support you through your mess, you're actually making it easier for them to love you well.

And someday, when they're going through their own crisis, you'll remember how they showed up for you, and you'll be able to show up for them in the same way. That's how friendship works - it's not always 50/50, but over time, it balances out.

Eventually, there will come a time when you need to start transitioning out of your toxic season. You'll know it's time when:

- You start having emotional energy to care about other people's problems again
- You start feeling more stable and capable of giving back

When that time comes, acknowledge what your friends did for you. Thank them. And then start slowly rebuilding those relationships into something more balanced. Start asking about their lives again. Start offering support when they need it. Start being the friend they were to you when you couldn't be a friend to anyone.

Scripture for When You Feel Guilty About Being Needy:

"Two are better than one, because they have a good return for their labor: If either of them falls down, one can help the other up." - Ecclesiastes 4:9-10

"Therefore encourage one another and build each other up, just as in fact you are doing." - 1 Thessalonians 5:11

Chapter 4: Music Can Soothe a Hurting Soul

Using music as a tool for healing

"You turned my wailing into dancing; you removed my sackcloth and clothed me with joy, that my heart may sing your praises and not be silent. Lord my God, I will praise you forever." - Psalm 30:11-12

I think most of us can relate that music affects us universally. You could be traveling around the world and may not understand the lyrics but you can get the sense and the mood by listening to music. Music is powerful. It has the ability to change our emotional state of mind. Well, let me share a little bit of what happened to me.

During my divorce journey, I was getting a lot of texts and a lot of support from people who would say "it's going to be okay." While that was kind and helpful, after a while I kept hearing "it's going to be okay" and I felt like it did not speak to my reality. It's not okay - you know what I'm going through is not okay right now! It's hard to focus on where it's going to be when right now hurts and is painful and is difficult.

So I texted a friend who I knew had been through a divorce and said, "Did you ever just get tired of people saying it's going to be okay?" Immediately I got a text back that said, "Listen to the song **Not Right Now**."

This is how crazy it is that I text someone and say "did you ever get tired of hearing it's going to be okay" and then this is the song they send. It's called "Not Right Now" by Jason Gray. It's on the album "Love Will Have the Final Word." The lyrics go:

"I know someday I know somehow I'll be okay but not right now, not right now... They want to tell me it'll be okay but that's not what I need

right now, not while my house is burning down... Don't tell me when I'm grieving that this happened for a reason, maybe one day we'll talk about the dreams that had to die for the new ones to come alive but not right now..."

I bought the album and I listened to this album every day for a year - the whole album. I knew without even knowing the author, the singer, I could tell he was either going through or had been through a divorce. I think at the time that I found the album he had not come out and told anyone that he'd been through a divorce, but I could tell because he just spoke the words that spoke to my pain.

I say get yourself a playlist. I warn you though - this time is so raw, so desperate. You may totally love a song during this period, but may not be able to listen to some of these songs later without going back to those feelings. I still need a little bit more space between my recovery journey and certain songs. So I warn you - if you're going to make a playlist you may not want to put your absolute favorite songs in there, but do put whatever speaks to you.

There is a song - I don't know why it just tickled me, it always makes me happy - the lyrics are "If you want to be happy for the rest of your life, never make a pretty woman your wife." I was like, that's my theme song! You know, find songs that make you happy, that help you escape, but also sometimes you need to find music that speaks to your situation.

I want to recommend "Love Will Have the Final Word" - almost every song on there definitely speaks to divorce recovery. There's a few on there that are more uplifting, but that album changed my life. It changed my perspective, it helped in my healing. It also taught me - they have a song on there about how to love someone else. It started me thinking, you know, okay, learning as I'm healing, learning how to love again, how to get to the places, how to touch people where they're hurting. Also to better understand what I might need for my own healing.

During this time, you're going to need different types of music:

Songs that validate your pain - Like "Not Right Now," these songs say what you're feeling when you can't find the words. They let you know you're not crazy for hurting this much.

Songs that make you smile - Even if it's something silly or random, if it makes you laugh or feel lighter for three minutes, put it on your list.

Songs that give you hope - Maybe not right now, but eventually you'll need songs that remind you there's still good ahead.

Worship songs that meet you where you are - Not the triumphant, everything-is-awesome worship, but the honest, "God I need You" kind of worship.

Listen, I get it. You're hurting and you want music that matches that hurt. But be careful not to get stuck in the really, really dark stuff. Yes, you need songs that understand your pain, but you also need to give yourself permission to laugh, to hope, to remember that there's still beauty in this world even when your world feels completely shattered.

Also, some songs are going to hit you out of nowhere. A song will come on the radio that you used to listen to with your ex, or that played at your wedding, or that represents some dream you had together. It's okay to turn it off. It's okay to cry. It's okay to let that song go for now.

Music is going to be one of your tools for healing, but like any tool, you get to decide how and when to use it.

Scripture for Your Playlist:

"He put a new song in my mouth, a hymn of praise to our God." -
Psalm 40:3

Chapter 5: Being Physical

Taking a hike and moving your body to heal your heart

"But those who hope in the Lord will renew their strength. They will soar on wings like eagles; they will run and not grow weary, they will walk and not be faint." - Isaiah 40:31

When Jeff and I were putting together this book, we were talking about our individual experiences - what worked for us, what didn't work for us, and what we wish somebody would have come and said to us. One of the things that we both found that we did individually was walking, and we did it in different ways for different reasons, but the conclusion was we found it very helpful.

His was more hiking, mine was more walking. I was in a place where I lived in my marital home, and I would walk from one room to the next and I would sort of feel - I'm going to use a word that expresses how I really felt - I would feel assaulted by memories and thoughts. I would walk through the dining room and think about our meals that we had there as a family, or an argument that took place. I would walk to the laundry room and see where we did a DIY project together. So I was sometimes bombarded by memories and thoughts that I didn't want to have and I didn't know what to do with it.

So I would just walk out my door. I would put on my shoes and I would walk out the door, and I had no destination in mind. I didn't know, I didn't even think "I'm going to go walk for my health" or "I'm going to go walk..." I was just fleeing my home and fleeing an emotional time.

There's something about forward motion that helps with emotional processing that I can't fully explain, but I know it works. When your thoughts are spinning in circles, when your emotions feel stuck, when you feel trapped by your circumstances, sometimes the simple act of putting one foot in front of the other can literally move you through it.

I would walk until I felt better, until I felt like I had my emotions more under control, until I realized that I could breathe. Actually, my attention would be focused - when I was leaving the home I was just frustrated, I was upset, I was stressed out. As I walked, you can't help but all your senses sort of kick in and you start seeing things and you start smelling things, you start hearing things, and then you start noticing that your hands are tingling or you're breathing hard, or "oh wow, my feet are hurting" or "oh my feet are not hurting."

It takes your attention off of the distress that you're under. Walking became my reset button. My escape hatch. My moving meditation.

Jeff's approach was different but equally effective. He would go hiking. He loves being in nature, and he would just get out and walk and not have any agenda in mind. He just found himself feeling so much better after he was done.

For him, hiking wasn't just about the physical movement - it was about getting away from civilization, from noise, from the constant reminders of normal life that felt anything but normal. It was about being in a place where he could think without interruption, where he could process his emotions without having to put on a brave face for anyone.

The physical challenge of hiking also gave him something to focus on besides his pain. When you're climbing a steep trail, you're not thinking about custody arrangements or dividing assets. You're thinking about where to put your next foot, how to regulate your breathing, whether you packed enough water.

It's amazing how therapeutic it can be to trade emotional challenges for physical ones, even temporarily.

Now, I can't bring all the science to you and tell you about how the blood flowing helps with mental health and being physically active helps us process things. Though I am sure that it's all true. But right now, this is a triage situation and I can only tell you what worked for me not why it did as we have stated many times Jeff and I are not experts in any field. This information is for you to benefit from our experience, if you only have five minutes to stop and listen to this - my friend, get out and walk.

Movement, especially rhythmic movement like walking, seems to have a meditative quality. Jeff and I both found that it gets you out of your head and into your body. It forces you to be present in the moment instead of spiraling through past regrets or future fears.

Walking outside adds another layer of getting out of your emotions and in to your senses we found. Fresh air, sunlight, nature - these all seem to be great benefits for our improved mental health. Being in natural settings helped us slow down rumination (that obsessively thinking about problems that goes nowhere). We also had the added benefit of lowering our blood pressure and we believed movement helped to reduce our anxiety.

Over the years we have truly come to believe and live by that there is something powerful about changing your physical environment when your emotional environment feels overwhelming. When the inside of your house feels suffocating, getting outside into open space can literally give you room to breathe. Which is how we took up hiking, kayaking, and other outdoor adventures.

Different Types of Movement for Different Needs

Not everyone is a walker or a hiker, and that's okay. The key is finding some form of physical movement that works for you and your situation.

Walking/Hiking: Great for processing thoughts, getting out of triggering environments, spending time in nature, and having low-impact exercise that almost anyone can do.

Running: Perfect if you need to burn off intense emotions like anger or anxiety. The rhythmic nature of running can be very meditative, and the endorphin release is significant.

Swimming: Excellent if you need to feel weightless for a while, if you want full-body exercise without joint impact, or if you find water soothing.

Dancing: Wonderful if you need to shake off emotions, if you want to connect with music (remember our music chapter?), or if you need to remember that your body can feel joy.

Yoga: Ideal if you need to reconnect your mind and body, if you want to combine movement with meditation, or if you need to release physical tension you're carrying.

Weightlifting: Great if you need to feel strong and capable, if you want to channel anger into something productive, or if you need the confidence boost that comes with getting physically stronger.

Gardening: Perfect if you want to nurture something while you're healing, if you need to feel connected to growth and renewal, or if you want gentle movement combined with being outdoors.

Cleaning/Organizing: Sounds weird, but sometimes vigorous cleaning can be incredibly therapeutic. It burns energy, creates visible progress, and gives you a sense of control when everything else feels chaotic.

Movement a Choice, Not a Chore

We found the difference between exercise that helps with emotional healing and exercise that feels like another burden is often in how you approach it.

We suggest you don't make it about weight loss or getting in shape or achieving some fitness goal. Make it about feeling better emotionally. Make it about getting out of your head. Make it about having something that's just for you.

Create little rituals around your movement time:

- Put on music that motivates you or soothes you
- Choose a scenic route that you enjoy
- Bring your phone and listen to podcasts or audiobooks
- Make it a time to pray or meditate
- Set a small goal (like walking to a certain landmark) and celebrate when you achieve it

For me, those walks became a form of prayer. I wasn't always consciously praying, but there was something about the rhythm of walking that opened up a space for God to meet me.

Sometimes I would cry as I walked, and it felt like God was walking with me through my tears. Sometimes I would feel angry and I would stomp along the sidewalk, and it felt like God could handle my anger. Sometimes I would feel peaceful for the first time all day, and it felt like God was giving me a little gift of relief.

There's something about being in motion that makes it easier to feel God's presence. Maybe it's because we're not sitting still long enough for our worries to catch up with us. Maybe it's because we're getting out of our own environments and into God's creation. Maybe it's because physical movement helps us get out of our heads and into our hearts, where God meets us.

I don't know the theology of it, but I know the experience of it. Some of my most meaningful encounters with God during my divorce happened while I was walking.

There's something deeply metaphorical about physical movement during divorce recovery. You are literally practicing the act of moving forward. You are proving to yourself, step by step, that you can keep going even when the path is unclear.

Every walk is practice for the longer journey of rebuilding your life. Every hike is proof that you can handle difficult terrain. Every workout is evidence that you're stronger than you think. The physical act of moving your body becomes a metaphor for the emotional and spiritual work of moving through grief, moving past anger, moving toward hope.

Some days, it might be the only forward motion you can manage. And that's enough.

Scripture for Movement:

"But those who hope in the Lord will renew their strength. They will soar on wings like eagles; they will run and not grow weary, they will walk and not be faint." - Isaiah 40:31

Chapter 6: Run to a MEGA Church

Finding your place in the body of Christ during crisis

"And let us consider how we may spur one another on toward love and good deeds, not giving up meeting together, as some are in the habit of doing, but encouraging one another—and all the more as you see the Day approaching." - Hebrews 10:24-25

One of the things that Jeff and I acknowledged when we were putting this book together is that we both felt alienated by our churches. And when I say church, I mean the body of Christ, not a particular building or a particular group of people. We just felt alienated from it because it's like the one place that you didn't want to run to and say, "Hey, I'm getting a divorce, help me," because most of the churches that we know - here in the South of the USA, - have programs for how to help your marriage, how to fix your marriage, how to save your marriage. However, we both were in situations where that was not an option of saving those marriages. We had to deal with the reality that we were going to get a divorce and that we still were Christians.

Jeff's story is he was involved in church but he switched churches around because it was just a time fraught with a lot of embarrassment, a lot of worry, a lot of concern, and not knowing who to talk to and where to go.

Let me be really honest about something that I think a lot of Christians going through divorce experience but don't talk about: church can feel like the least safe place to be when your marriage is falling apart. You walk into a building full of families sitting together in neat little rows. You hear sermons about God's design for marriage and family. You see happy couples holding hands during worship. You participate in small groups where everyone talks about their spouse and their kids like life is just going according to plan.

And there you are, feeling like a walking contradiction of everything the church preaches about marriage and family. You start to wonder if people are looking at you differently. You wonder if they're whispering about you in the parking lot. You wonder if they think less of you, if they think you didn't try hard enough, if they think you're somehow less of a Christian because your marriage didn't make it.

Maybe some of them do think those things. Maybe some of them don't know how to handle the messiness of real life. Maybe some churches really aren't equipped to deal with the reality that sometimes marriages end, even among people who love Jesus.

But here's what I want you to hear: you cannot do this alone. You cannot heal in isolation. You cannot rebuild your life without community. And the church - the body of Christ - is still your family, even when your family of origin has been shattered.

I know it's tempting to pull away from church when you're going through a divorce. I know it feels easier to just stay home on Sunday mornings, to avoid the questions and the stares and the awkwardness. But isolation is not your friend during this time. Isolation allows your thoughts to spiral. Isolation lets shame and guilt grow unchecked. Isolation convinces you that you're the only person who's ever been through this, that you're beyond help, that God is done with you.

None of that is true, but it's hard to remember that when you're sitting alone in your house every Sunday morning. You need to be around people who are worshiping God even when you don't feel like you can worship. You need to be in the presence of others who are declaring God's goodness even when your life feels like evidence to the contrary. You need to hear testimonies of God's faithfulness from people who have walked through their own valleys.

You need corporate worship because sometimes other people have to do the singing and praying for you when you can't do it for yourself.

Here's how I used church, and the one piece of advice I'm going to give you is: run to your church. Go to your church. This is not the time to shy away from them. You cannot do this alone. You need community and you need your church and you need to give your church the opportunity to support you. Don't assume they're going to shun you away. Don't assume they're not going to understand or they're not going to come alongside you and walk with you through this. Give them the opportunity to be there.

But if you can't go to your local church - maybe the person that you're getting divorced from goes there, maybe all your family goes there, maybe the minute you walk in the door everybody knows all your business and you don't feel comfortable going there - then for a time, take a time out.

Here's what I highly recommend, and this is what I did: I went and found the biggest church in my community and I went to it because I didn't want anybody asking me anything. I wanted to just go hear and worship God. I wanted to go to a place where I could be fed, and that was it.

It was a very selfish time for me where I didn't go to try to help anybody. I just wanted to be anonymous.

So I found the biggest church I could find where I could just sneak in the side door and sit there and still be a part of corporate worship. When I didn't feel like singing, when I didn't feel like worshiping God, I was still in the presence of those that could do it for me.

That is what corporate worship - that's one of the reasons I love when the music program is important - because they are sometimes the voice for us who don't have that talent, but also for us that are maybe hurting so badly that you can't sing to the Lord, and yet you can still be in the presence of someone doing it for you.

I went as an anonymous person and I sat there and I didn't have to worry because there were so many people there, they didn't know if I was there all the time or they didn't know, "Wait a minute, that's part of a family unit - where's the rest of her family?" They didn't know anything about me and they didn't bother me. They said hello and hi and went on about their business, and that's what I needed during that time.

I was able to hear the word of God. I was able to be a part of a family, the body of Christ, and yet not having to deal with what was going on in my life at that time. I could just go there and worship God.

So I say, I don't want you to leave your church if it's working for you and if it's supporting you during this time, then most definitely do it. But if you are on the fence of "Oh, I can't go to my church, I can't deal with it, I don't want to deal with all the questions of everyone to even worship and enjoy church," then I say go find the biggest church in your community you can find and just sit and be.

We say a lot of negative things about mega churches, but this right here is where mega churches can excel in healing and helping people - allowing people just to be in the presence of God and worshiping with others and feel normal for a little bit.

You know, just go there and everyone's on the same playing field. The lights go down and we're just there to worship God. We're not there to look at what we're wearing, we're not there to look at all the family units, we're not there to look at what we have or don't have. We're just there to worship God and let Him love on us, let Him let people pray for us.

There's something beautiful about being in a room with hundreds of other people who are all declaring that God is good, even when your personal circumstances are screaming the opposite. There's something powerful about hearing a room full of voices singing about God's faithfulness when your faith is hanging by a thread.

In a mega church, you can:

- Slip in late and leave early without anyone noticing
- Sit in the back and cry without drawing attention
- Receive prayer without having to explain your whole story
- Hear God's word without fielding questions about your personal life
- Experience worship without having to perform happiness
- Feel part of something bigger than your problems

Now, having said all that about mega churches, let me also say this: if you go to a church, give them the opportunity to support you before you just say no, they're not going to support me in this, they're not going to understand my situation.

Give them the opportunity. At least go to your pastor and give him the opportunity to be the body of Christ for you. And if not, if you don't get the support that you need, then run to the biggest mega church you can find and just be anonymous and worship God.

Some of the most beautiful stories I've heard from people going through divorce have come from churches that stepped up in amazing ways:

- The small group that brought meals for two months
- The women's ministry that surrounded a newly divorced mom with practical support and friendship
- The congregation that continued to treat both ex-spouses with love and respect
- The church that started a divorce recovery ministry because they realized how much it was needed

Your church might surprise you. They might be more gracious, more understanding, more supportive than you expect. But you have to give them the chance.

Creating Your Own Church Community

Sometimes you might need to create your own version of church community for a while. This might look like:

Small group with other divorced Christians: Meeting regularly to study Scripture, pray together, and support each other through the unique challenges of divorce recovery.

Online church community: If you can't find what you need locally, there are online communities and even online church services that might meet your needs temporarily.

Multi-church approach: Maybe you attend Sunday service at the mega church for anonymity, but go to small group at a smaller church where you can build relationships.

Here's something I want you to consider: your presence in church during your divorce recovery is actually a gift to the church, even if it doesn't feel like it.

You are showing other people that it's possible to love God even when life falls apart. You are demonstrating that faith isn't dependent on having a perfect family. You are giving permission to other people who are struggling to be honest about their pain instead of pretending everything is fine.

Your willingness to keep showing up, to keep seeking God, to keep believing that He loves you even when your life looks nothing like what you planned - that's a powerful testimony.

The church needs people like you. They need to see that God's love is bigger than traditional family structures. They need to learn how to support people in crisis. They need to be reminded that the Gospel is for broken people, not just people who have it all together.

Your presence is a gift, even when it feels like you're the one who needs all the gifts.

Scriptures for Church Community:

"Bear one another's burdens, and so fulfill the law of Christ." - Galatians 6:2

"As iron sharpens iron, so one person sharpens another." - Proverbs 27:17

"And let us consider how to stir up one another to love and good works, not neglecting to meet together." - Hebrews 10:24-25

END OF PART ONE: SURVIVAL MODE

My friend, if you've made it through these first six chapters, I want you to stop and take a deep breath. Look how far you've come. You've learned to feel your pain without drowning in it, you've found safe people and safe places, you've given yourself permission to be needy, and you've stayed connected to God and His people even when it was hard.

This is huge. This is survival, and survival is victory right now.

Before you move into the next section, I need you to hear this: there is no timeline for this part. Some people need weeks here, some need months, some need a full year. There's no award for speed, and there's no shame in taking your time. You stay in survival mode as long as you need to survive.

How do you know if you're ready for recovery mode? When you can get through most days without feeling like you're drowning. When the crisis has passed and you're not just reacting anymore. When you can think about your future without panic setting in.

If that's not you yet, that's perfectly okay. Go back through these chapters again. Keep using these tools. Keep leaning on your people. Keep hiding in God's Word. You'll know when you're ready to take the next step, and when you are, I'll be here waiting for you.

Part Two: Recovery

Chapter 7: Embrace Your New Reality

The turning point of acceptance

"Therefore, if anyone is in Christ, the new creation has come: The old has gone, the new is here!" - 2 Corinthians 5:17

We're moving from survival mode to recovery now. This one is kind of a tough one. This one really is the difference between moving into recovery or going back to survival mode. It is necessary as it is embracing your new reality.

For some of us, divorce is forced upon us. Divorce wasn't an option as there is no other option, it is what it is. And accepting that - and that's why this is really titled for Christians because that's hard. Coming through life as a Christian, I don't know anyone who gets married and says, "Well, I can always just get divorced." You get married and you are in a committed relationship and you know that life is going to come at you. You know there's ups, there's downs. You are interlocked with someone and you build a life with them and you build a future with them.

Having to stop and accept the fact that that is over and that there's a divorce, there's an ending of that whole, not only that life but the future of that life, is difficult. It's not an easy step, but it is a necessary step.

The first six chapters were about triage - stopping the bleeding, getting you through the immediate crisis, helping you survive the initial shock and trauma. Those chapters were about reaction - reacting to something that happened to you.

But this chapter marks a turning point. This is where you move from reacting to being proactive. This is where you stop being a victim of your circumstances and start taking some control over your response to those circumstances.

It's like waking up from a coma and realizing you need physical therapy. You accept the fact that your arm is hurt - I don't know how you go from a coma to having a hurt arm, but we're gonna go with it - because the truth is, it is your time now. It is your time to embrace your new reality, to accept it, and then to turn the page and start being proactive in your recovery.

But you can't do that until you embrace the fact that this is your new reality.

Let me be clear about what I mean when I say "embrace your new reality," because I'm not talking about being happy about it. I'm not talking about pretending it's what you wanted. I'm not talking about putting on a brave face and acting like everything is fine.

Embracing your new reality means:

- Stopping the fight against what is
- Accepting that this is actually happening, not just a bad dream you'll wake up from
- Acknowledging that your old life, your old plans, your old future is gone
- Recognizing that denial is keeping you stuck
- Choosing to work with your current circumstances instead of against them
- Moving from "this shouldn't be happening" to "this is happening, now what?"

It's the difference between spending your energy trying to go back to something that no longer exists and spending your energy building something new with what you have now.

Let me tell you about some of the ways that I decided to embrace my new reality. These may seem silly to you - you don't have to do them. You may try a few things and then finally come up with something else that works. But for me, taking off my wedding rings was significant. It was a way that I outwardly was telling the world the truth. Being honest with myself was the first step, the first way that I decided to embrace my new reality.

Another way was - and again this might seem silly to you - but I put the pillows in the middle of the bed. I was like, "I'm taking over the whole bed. This is my bed. There's only one person that sleeps in this bed." That was just a way to help myself accept my new reality and embrace it and say, "Okay, this is my new truth. This is my next story. This is the next chapter in my story."

Another way is I used to keep my hair really, really short and I let my hair really grow. I stopped cutting it. It got very, very long through these years of this time of recovery, but it was just a way that I was letting new growth happen. It was an outward show, an outward expression of the fact that I was embracing a new life, a new me.

Some people go buy new vehicles. Some people change their names. Whatever you need to do - and you don't have to do anything outwardly. It could all be done inwardly. But you do have to take that moment where you take a deep breath and you accept: "This is my new reality. This is a truth that I have to accept." And acceptance is key to survival.

Once you accept it, I'm telling you, it is a hard step, but it is the key that unlocks a possible future for you.

I want to make something really clear here: accepting your new reality doesn't mean you approve of it. It doesn't mean you think it's good or right or fair. It doesn't mean you're not angry about it or sad about it. Acceptance is not the same as approval.

You can accept that your marriage is over while still believing marriage should be permanent. You can accept that you're getting divorced while still believing divorce is not God's ideal plan. You can accept your new circumstances while still grieving what you've lost. Acceptance is simply acknowledging what is true. It's stopping the exhausting work of fighting reality and redirecting that energy toward dealing with reality.

Think of it this way: if you're in a car accident, you can spend your energy being angry that the accident happened, or you can spend your energy getting medical help and figuring out how to heal. Both responses are understandable, but only one of them helps you move forward.

Acceptance is choosing to focus on what you can control going forward rather than what you couldn't control that already happened.

As Christians, we're taught that God can do anything. We're taught to have faith, to believe in miracles, to never give up hope. And those are good things. But sometimes they can make it harder to accept difficult realities.

You might be thinking:

- "If I accept this divorce, does that mean I'm giving up on God's ability to restore my marriage?"
- "If I embrace this new reality, does that mean I'm not trusting God for a miracle?"
- "If I stop praying for reconciliation, does that mean I lack faith?"

Let me suggest a different way to think about it: maybe accepting your new reality is actually an act of faith. Maybe it's trusting that God can work in your life even when it looks different than you planned. Maybe it's believing that God's love for you isn't dependent on your marital status.

Maybe embracing your new reality is saying, "God, I don't understand why this happened, but I trust that You can still do good things in my life, even in this situation I never wanted."

Accepting your new reality isn't just a mental exercise - it often requires practical steps. Here are some things that might be part of your acceptance process:

Legal steps: Filing divorce papers, meeting with lawyers, dividing assets. These make the divorce legally real.

Living situation steps: Moving out, changing your address, setting up your own household. These make the separation physically real.

Financial steps: Opening your own bank account, creating a budget for one income, changing beneficiaries. These make the financial reality concrete.

Social steps: Telling friends and family, changing your relationship status, attending events alone. These make the change public.

Identity steps: Taking off your wedding ring, changing your name back, updating your emergency contacts. These reflect your new identity.

Future planning steps: Making new goals, changing your retirement plans, thinking about dating again. These acknowledge that you have a future that doesn't include your ex.

Each of these steps can be emotionally difficult, but they're also steps toward freedom. Each one moves you a little further from denial and a little closer to acceptance.

There's something powerful about making physical changes that reflect your inner reality. It's a way of telling yourself and the world that you're not the same person you were before. Some people completely redecorate their homes. Some people move to a new city.

Some people get tattoos or piercings. Some people lose weight or get in shape. Some people go back to school or change careers.

The specific change doesn't matter as much as the symbolism: "I am not who I was before. I am becoming someone new." For me, growing my hair out was symbolic of letting new things grow in my life. Rearranging the bedroom was symbolic of making the space mine. Taking off my wedding ring was symbolic of being honest about my new relationship status.

Acceptance isn't usually a one-time event - it's a process that happens over time. You might have moments of acceptance followed by moments of denial. You might accept some aspects of your new reality while still fighting others.

That's normal. Healing isn't linear. Some days you'll wake up and think, "I can do this. I can build a good life as a single person." Other days you'll wake up and think, "This can't be my life. This can't be how my story goes."

Both of those feelings are valid. The goal isn't to never have moments of denial or grief. The goal is to have more moments of acceptance than denial, and to keep moving in the direction of embracing what is rather than fighting what isn't.

Here's why this step is so crucial: you cannot build a new life while you're still trying to resurrect your old one. You cannot move forward while you're facing backward. You cannot embrace new opportunities while your hands are still clinging to what's already gone.

Acceptance makes possible:

- Making plans for your actual future instead of your imaginary future
- Investing energy in what you can change instead of what you can't
- Building new relationships instead of waiting for old ones to be restored

- Developing new skills and interests instead of maintaining old routines
- Finding new sources of joy instead of mourning old sources of happiness
- Discovering new aspects of yourself instead of only identifying with your former roles

Acceptance is the foundation for everything else in your recovery. Without it, you're building on sand.

There's a strange kind of freedom that comes with accepting difficult realities. When you stop fighting what is, you free up enormous amounts of energy that you can redirect toward building what could be.

You can spend energy on:

- Figuring out what you want your life to look like now
- Developing new interests and relationships
- Building new skills and habits
- Creating new routines and traditions
- Planning a future that's actually possible

The energy you've been spending on resistance can be redirected toward rebuilding.

I want to make sure you understand the difference between acceptance and resignation, because they're not the same thing. Resignation is passive. It's giving up. It's saying, "I guess this is just how my life is going to be and there's nothing I can do about it."

Acceptance is active. It's choosing to work with your circumstances instead of against them. It's saying, "This is how my life is now, and I'm going to make the best of it." Resignation leads to bitterness and depression. Acceptance leads to hope and new possibilities.

Don't resign yourself to a miserable life. Accept your new reality so you can build a good life within it.

For Christians, acceptance can be a deeply spiritual act. It can be a way of saying to God, "I don't understand Your plan, but I trust Your heart. I don't like what's happened, but I believe You can still work good in my life."

It can be an act of surrender - not the kind of surrender that gives up on life, but the kind that gives up the illusion of control and trusts God with the unknown future. Some of my deepest spiritual growth happened when I finally stopped fighting my new reality and started asking God, "What do You want to do in my life now? How do You want to use this experience? Who do You want me to become through this?"

Those are questions you can only ask after you've accepted what is.

If you've been stuck in denial for a long time and can't seem to move toward acceptance, you might need professional help. A good counselor can help you work through whatever is keeping you stuck.

Sometimes we resist acceptance because:

- We're afraid of what it means about us
- We're afraid of the future
- We feel like accepting means we're giving up on God
- We're not sure who we are outside of our former identity
- We're afraid of being alone
- We're terrified of starting over

These are all valid fears, and sometimes you need professional help to work through them. There's no shame in getting help to move through this crucial step in your healing.

Remember, Jeff and I are not licensed professionals. We're just sharing what worked for us. If you need more help than simple tips and encouragement, please seek out qualified counselors or therapists.

Scripture for Acceptance:

"And we know that in all things God works for the good of those who love him, who have been called according to his purpose." - Romans 8:28

"Trust in the Lord with all your heart and lean not on your own understanding." - Proverbs 3:5

Chapter 8: Honor Yourself

Celebrating how far you've come

"She is clothed with strength and dignity; she can laugh at the days to come." - Proverbs 31:25

There is a point in this journey when you're going through divorce and you are really needy - you think everything's about you and you feel so tender, like you're very thin-skinned and it's a lot of pain. Eventually there will come a time when you go into recovery mode as you have accepted your reality, you're allowing others to help you, and now you are ready to honor yourself.

At this point you say, "I'm okay right here where I am. I've made it this far. I've made it to today - whatever today is. I've made it this far." This is a process, it is a journey. It is not something you can just overnight accept and deal with and recover from. It's a journey and this chapter is all about that next step when you stop and you honor yourself.

If you're like most people going through divorce, the idea of "honoring yourself" probably feels weird, selfish, or even wrong. You might be thinking:

- "I don't deserve to be honored - my marriage failed"
- "I've made too many mistakes to celebrate anything"
- "Other people have it worse than me"
- "I should be focused on my kids/healing/getting my life together, not celebrating"
- "Honoring myself feels prideful"

Let me tell you something: these thoughts are exactly why you need this chapter.

We live in a culture that's really good at pointing out what we're doing wrong, what we need to improve, how we're falling short. We're experts at criticism and amateurs at celebration. This is especially true when we're going through difficult times.

But here's what I've learned: you cannot heal properly without acknowledging your own strength. You cannot move forward without recognizing how far you've come. You cannot build a healthy future without honoring the person who survived to build it.

When I talk about honoring yourself, I'm not talking about thinking you're perfect or pretending you haven't made mistakes. I'm not talking about pride or arrogance or thinking you're better than anyone else.

I'm talking about acknowledging the truth about your journey:

- You have survived something that could have destroyed you
- You have kept going when stopping would have been easier
- You have faced pain that most people can't imagine
- You have made difficult decisions that required courage
- You have gotten up every day and tried to do the next right thing
- You are still here, still fighting, still hoping

That deserves to be acknowledged. That deserves to be honored.

You have to look back and just give yourself some grace, give yourself some kindness. I guarantee you at some point you have said something wrong, you have done something wrong, you've had the wrong attitude, you have missed an opportunity. Divorce is a highly emotionally charged time and event in your life, and we are not going to manage that perfectly. We are human and we make mistakes, and we sin all the time, and we most definitely sin when there's a lot of emotions involved.

So you have to at this point give yourself some grace and give others grace in your situation, but mainly today is about honoring yourself.

Let me tell you about some of the mistakes I made during my divorce:

- I said things in anger that I regret
- I made decisions based on emotion rather than wisdom
- I involved my children in adult conversations they shouldn't have heard
- I talked badly about my ex to people who didn't need to hear it
- I spent money I didn't have trying to make myself feel better
- I isolated myself when I should have reached out for help
- I trusted some people I shouldn't have and didn't trust some people I should have

I could spend all my time focusing on those mistakes, beating myself up for not handling things perfectly. Or I can acknowledge that I was doing the best I could with the tools I had at the time, in the most difficult circumstances of my life. That doesn't excuse the mistakes, but it puts them in context. And it allows me to learn from them without being destroyed by them.

Here's something I wish someone had told me during my divorce: you don't have to be perfect to be worthy of love and respect. You don't have to handle everything gracefully to deserve kindness. You don't have to make all the right decisions to be a good person.

You just have to be human. And being human means being flawed, making mistakes, learning as you go, and doing better when you know better. The same grace you would give to a friend going through divorce, give that to yourself. The same compassion you would show to your child if they were struggling, show that to yourself. The same understanding you would have for anyone else walking through this difficult journey, offer that to yourself.

You deserve the same kindness from yourself that you would give to anyone else in your situation.

So how do you actually honor yourself? How do you celebrate progress when everything still feels hard? How do you acknowledge your strength when you feel weak?

Treat yourself. Go buy yourself something special, something nice. My sister brought me a scarf and said, "Here's your happy divorce scarf." It wasn't that she was saying, "Oh, I'm so happy you got a divorce." She was saying, "I'm honoring this reality in your life and I'm honoring you, and I'm giving you something to smile about and cheer. I'm in this moment with you, but I'm also honoring what you've gone through and what you're going through."

I want to encourage you - go buy yourself a gift. If you're supporting someone by reading this, go buy them a gift. You don't have to say "happy divorce" - I took it the way my sister meant it, and it was sweet and wonderful, and I love that scarf and I still have it because it helped me even more accept that this was my reality. And not only that, it helped me see that others were going to accept it too, that I didn't have to walk around with my head held down in shame the rest of my life. It was just a fact and a truth.

Have a cup of coffee. It doesn't have to be a great big thing. Some people go on vacation, some people have what they call a midlife crisis and they change things significantly. But I think it could be just simple - just taking five minutes out of your day and saying, "Okay, I've done it. I'm surviving. I am doing the best I can. I'm gonna give myself some Grace. I'm making it through this situation. I'm trying to make the best of the situation. I've made mistakes, but I'm doing it. I'm continuing to push forward to be a better person and dealing with this to the best of my ability." Just honor yourself.

Do something significant. I like the idea of doing something significant to honor yourself. Go find a hike you really want to do, or run a three-mile race (I can't, but you know what I'm saying), or do something significant to just embrace that you have made it this far, that you are still alive, you're still doing it, you're still surviving.

I feel pretty certain there is some actual science behind why celebration and positive acknowledgment help with healing and recovery. Yet as we know Jeff nor I are professionals that can give you those kind of facts but we can tell you what we experienced:

You build confidence for future challenges. When you acknowledge what you've already survived, you build evidence for yourself that you can handle whatever comes next.

You shift your focus from what's wrong to what's working. This doesn't mean ignoring problems, but it means developing a more balanced perspective that includes both struggles and strengths.

You practice gratitude. Honoring yourself is a form of gratitude - being grateful for your own resilience, your own courage, your own commitment to keep going.

You model healthy self-relationship for others. If you have children, they're watching how you treat yourself during difficult times. If you show yourself kindness and respect, you're teaching them to do the same.

People honor their progress in different ways, and what works for you might be completely different from what worked for Jeff and I. Here are some ideas:

Symbolic gestures:

- Buy yourself jewelry that represents your new chapter
- Get a tattoo that symbolizes your strength (if that's your thing)
- Plant a tree or garden to represent new growth
- Treat yourself to an acoustic guitar (like Jeff did)
- Write yourself a letter acknowledging your courage

Experiential honors:

- Take a trip you've always wanted to take
- Try something you've never done before
- Take a class you've been interested in
- Join a group or activity you've been considering
- Go to that restaurant or show you've been wanting to try

Service-oriented honors:

- Volunteer for a cause that matters to you

- Mentor someone else going through divorce
- Use your skills to help others
- Start or join a support group
- Share your story to encourage others

Personal development honors:

- Invest in therapy or counseling for yourself
- Take a class or workshop for personal growth
- Read books that inspire and encourage you
- Start a new hobby or revisit an old one
- Set new goals for your future

Simple daily honors:

- Take a long bath with candles
- Sleep in on Saturday morning
- Buy yourself flowers
- Make your favorite meal
- Spend an afternoon doing exactly what you want to do

I want to make sure you understand the difference between honoring your progress and hiding from your problems. Honoring yourself doesn't mean:

- Pretending everything is fine when it's not
- Avoiding the work you still need to do
- Ignoring ongoing problems or responsibilities
- Using celebration as a way to avoid difficult emotions
- Spending money you don't have to make yourself feel better temporarily

Healthy self-honoring acknowledges both your progress AND your ongoing journey. It celebrates how far you've come while remaining realistic about the work still ahead. It's saying, "I've made it this far AND I still have work to do" rather than "I've made it this far SO I don't have any more work to do."

If you're struggling with the idea of honoring yourself because it feels selfish, let me remind you of something: taking care of yourself isn't selfish - it's necessary. You cannot pour from an empty cup. You cannot give strength you don't have. You cannot encourage others if you're constantly discouraging yourself.

When you honor your own progress and strength:

- You have more energy to invest in your children, your work, your relationships
- You model healthy self-respect for others
- You build the confidence needed to make good decisions going forward
- You create emotional reserves that help you handle future challenges
- You become someone who can support others instead of always needing support

Taking care of yourself isn't taking away from others - it's ensuring you have something valuable to offer them.

Honoring yourself isn't a one-time event - it's an ongoing practice that becomes part of how you relate to yourself. As you continue to heal and grow, you'll want to continue acknowledging your progress, celebrating your wins, and treating yourself with kindness.

This might look like:

- Regular check-ins with yourself about how you're doing
- Celebrating anniversaries of important milestones
- Acknowledging when you handle something better than you would have before
- Treating yourself kindly when you make mistakes
- Setting boundaries that protect your well-being
- Making choices that reflect your worth and value

Learning to honor yourself during divorce recovery can actually be one of the unexpected gifts of this difficult journey. Many people discover during this process that they've been way too hard on themselves for years, and learning to be kinder to themselves becomes a life-changing skill. When you honor yourself appropriately, you teach important lessons to the people around you:

Your children learn that it's possible to go through difficult times without losing your sense of worth. They learn that mistakes don't define you, that resilience is possible, that self-respect is important.

Your friends and family learn how to support people going through crisis. They see that celebration and acknowledgment can coexist with struggle and pain.

Other people facing similar challenges learn that survival is possible, that healing happens gradually, that strength can be found even in weakness.

You teach yourself that you are worthy of kindness, that your efforts matter, that your journey has value even when it's not perfect.

Looking back on my divorce recovery, the times when I honored myself and acknowledged my progress were turning points in my healing. When my sister gave me that scarf, when I decided to let my hair grow, when I rearranged my bedroom - these weren't just superficial changes. They were ways of saying to myself and the world, "I am not the same person I was before. I am becoming someone new. And that person deserves respect and kindness."

It took me a while to learn this. In the beginning, I was so focused on what I had lost, what I had done wrong, how far I had to go, that I couldn't see the strength it was taking just to keep going. I couldn't see that getting up every day and taking care of my responsibilities was actually a heroic act.

But as I started to acknowledge my own courage, my own resilience, my own growth, something shifted. I started to believe that I could not just survive this experience, but actually thrive because of it. I started to see myself as someone who was stronger than I had ever imagined, more capable than I had ever believed.

That shift in self-perception changed everything. It gave me permission to dream new dreams, to set new goals, to believe that my best days might actually be ahead of me instead of behind me.

So today, my friend, I want to invite you to honor yourself. Pat yourself on the back. Go get yourself some chocolate if you want some. But honor yourself - you are doing it. You're reading this book, you're doing what it takes, you're doing the work, you're doing the hard stuff, and you will make it into thriving.

Take a moment right now to acknowledge:

- You woke up today even though yesterday was hard
- You are actively working on your healing instead of giving up
- You are seeking help and resources instead of suffering alone
- You are taking care of your responsibilities even when you don't feel like it
- You are still believing in the possibility of a good future
- You are showing up for your life even when it looks nothing like what you planned

That is extraordinary. That is heroic. That deserves to be honored.

So honor yourself today. Do something kind for yourself. Acknowledge your own courage. Celebrate your own resilience. You've earned it.

Scripture for Self-Honor:

"I praise you because I am fearfully and wonderfully made; your works are wonderful, I know that full well." - Psalm 139:14

"But he said to me, 'My grace is sufficient for you, for my power is made perfect in weakness.'" - 2 Corinthians 12:9

Chapter 9: Help Others Help You

Being honest about what you need

"Carry each other's burdens, and in this way you will fulfill the law of Christ." - Galatians 6:2

It's interesting - when you're going through a divorce, it impacts not just you. It impacts your friend group, it impacts your parents, your former spouse's parents, in-laws. I mean, Aunts, Uncles, kids, nieces, nephews - a divorce impacts your whole group, your whole network, your whole social network.

There comes a point in time during survival - it's really a time for you to take care of you and be a little toxic as we talked about in an earlier chapter. When you start moving into recovery, you've accepted the fact that there is a divorce, and now it's time to kind of move into helping others help you.

In this chapter, I want to talk a little bit about how you can do that, and one of those is by being honest - just being honest with everyone in a way that is authentic and in a way that is also self-protective. When I say be honest, I don't mean tell everybody everything. I don't mean everyone is entitled to know all your business and what's happening. I don't believe that at all. I believe that you need to say what is appropriate based on the level of intimacy in the relationship.

Let me tell you something about divorce that nobody warns you about: it doesn't just affect you and your ex-spouse. It sends shockwaves through your entire social network. Everyone who cared about you as a couple is now trying to figure out how to relate to you as individuals.

Your parents are grieving the loss of their daughter-in-law or son-in-law. Your children are trying to navigate a completely changed family structure. Your mutual friends are wondering if they have to choose sides. Your coworkers are unsure whether to mention it or pretend nothing happened. Your neighbors don't know if they should ask how you're doing or give you space.

Everyone wants to help, but nobody knows how. Everyone cares, but nobody knows what to say. Everyone can see you're struggling, but nobody wants to make it worse by doing the wrong thing. And meanwhile, you're drowning in your own pain and trying to figure out how to manage everyone else's discomfort with your situation.

That's exhausting. It's overwhelming. And it's completely unnecessary if you learn how to help others help you.

Most people have never been through a divorce themselves, so they literally don't know what you need. They're operating from their own fears and assumptions about what divorce must be like. Some people are afraid to bring it up because they don't want to make you sad. (Newsflash: you're already sad. They're not going to make you sad by acknowledging it.)

Some people want to fix it and get frustrated when they realize they can't. They want to give you advice or solutions when what you really need is just someone to listen. Some people are uncomfortable with pain and don't know how to be around someone who's hurting. They either avoid you completely or try to cheer you up when you need to grieve.

Some people are worried about saying the wrong thing, so they end up saying nothing at all, which feels like abandonment to you. Some people take your divorce personally, like it's a threat to their own marriage, and they respond with judgment or distance.

None of this is about you - it's about their own discomfort, their own fears, their own lack of experience with crisis. But the result is that you end up feeling isolated and unsupported when you need community the most.

Here's what I've learned: most people genuinely want to help, they just don't know how. And when people don't know how to help, they either do nothing (which feels like abandonment) or they do the wrong thing (which feels hurtful).

But when you help people help you by being specific about what you need, suddenly they have a roadmap. They know how to show love to you in a way that actually feels loving.

Instead of leaving people to guess what you need, tell them:

"I don't need advice right now, I just need you to listen."

"I need practical help - could you bring dinner Tuesday night?"

"I need distraction - want to go see a funny movie with me?"

"I need to talk about something other than my divorce for a while."

"I need you to check on me regularly because I tend to isolate myself when I'm struggling."

"I need you to include me in normal activities so I don't feel like my divorce defines me."

"I need you to be patient with me while I figure out who I am as a single person."

When you're specific about what you need, you give people the gift of knowing how to love you well.

Like your parents, you might want to let them know more than you would let your neighbor. Your neighbor's wondering what's going on, so it's just time to let others help you by being honest about what you're going through.

I highly recommend tailoring a nice, to-the-point message and just letting everyone know what's going on. Not announcing, but just "here's what's going on, here's how you can support my family, my children, and what's going on" because when people don't know, they make things up.

One way to also help lower the drama and ensure that there is no story is to just put out there enough information that's necessary.

Here's how I think about levels of intimacy and information sharing:

Inner circle (closest family and friends): These people get the full story. They know the details, the timeline, the challenges you're facing. They're the ones you call when you're having a breakdown at 2 AM.

Close friends and family: These people get the basic facts and updates. They know you're getting divorced, when it will be final, how the kids are doing, what your major needs are.

Acquaintances and coworkers: These people get the simple facts. "We've decided to divorce. It's been difficult, but we're working through it. Thank you for your concern."

Public/social media: This gets the most basic announcement if you choose to make one at all. "After much consideration, [Name] and I have decided to divorce. We appreciate your prayers during this difficult time."

The key is being intentional about what you share with whom, rather than either oversharing with everyone or hiding from everyone.

We live in an age where social media is how we communicate with each other. There was a lot of people who used to air all their dirty laundry out on Facebook - people would talk and be like, "Oh, they shouldn't be saying all that on Facebook." But I also think there is a respectful way to let everybody know what's going on, allow them to absorb it without being in front of you, and I think that is being honest but yet also removes you from their shock and how they feel about it.

I really think tailoring a nice, to-the-point message on social media and just saying "here's what's going on" - not announcing, but just letting people know what's happening. This can help your kids when they go to school because kids hear their parents talking and then they'll ask your child about it. Being a child, they'll ask your child, "I heard this, my mama said that," and I just think it's so much easier if you just go ahead and do a carefully thought-out, constructed post.

I know that's controversial, so that's just an idea, that's just my take on it. There are other people - like Jeff- who never told anyone and just let people assume whatever they wanted to for many, many years. It was years before anyone knew that he was actually divorced. That was his way of dealing with it. He had accepted his reality and he said, "I became a hermit and didn't let anyone know what I was dealing with. I suffered a long time in silence, alone." Years later, Jeff realized it would have benefitted him to let others in on his true situation. Which is why he helped create this book for you.

Whereas I was more of a social person and so I felt the need to let people know. My ex and I did not make a joint statement even though I wanted to - I felt the need to let people know. That's why I'm saying, based on that experience, I wish that I had made some sort of to the point message, because I think I would have gotten more support from people if they had known what I was going through.

When you're honest about your situation (at the appropriate level for each relationship), several good things happen:

People stop wondering and making up stories. When there's an information vacuum, people fill it with speculation. Usually, the speculation is worse than the truth.

People know how to respond to you. Instead of avoiding you because they don't know what to say, they can offer appropriate support.

You get the help you actually need. Instead of people guessing what might help, they can provide what you've specifically requested.

You feel less isolated. When you're honest about your struggles, you often discover that other people have been through similar things.

You model healthy communication. You show others that it's possible to go through difficult times without hiding or falling apart completely.

You give permission to others to be honest about their struggles. Your vulnerability often helps others feel safe to share their own difficulties.

There's a difference between being honest and oversharing. Honesty is sharing appropriate information to help people understand your situation and support you well. Oversharing is dumping all your emotions and details on people who aren't equipped to handle them.

Honest: "We've decided to divorce. It's been really difficult, and I'm taking it one day at a time."

Oversharing: "He cheated on me with his secretary and then had the nerve to ask for alimony, and I found out because I saw the text messages when I was looking through his phone, which I know I shouldn't have done but I had this feeling..."

Honest: "I'm struggling with some depression and anxiety right now, so I might not be myself for a while."

Oversharing: "I'm on three different medications and I cry every day and I haven't been sleeping and yesterday I had a panic attack in the grocery store..."

Honest: "The kids are having a hard time adjusting, so we'd appreciate prayers for our family."

Oversharing: "My daughter is acting out at school and my son won't talk to his father and they're both in therapy but it's not working and I don't know what to do..."

The difference is in the level of detail and the emotional intensity. Honest sharing gives people the information they need to support you. Oversharing overwhelms people with more information than they can process or help with and later you will regret being an oversharer as I certainly have.

Again, most people want to help, but they need you to tell them how. Here are some specific ways you can help others help you:

Practical support:

- "Could you pick up groceries for me this week?"
- "Would you mind carpooling my kids to soccer practice for the next month?"
- "I'm struggling to keep up with housework - would you be willing to help me clean this weekend?"
- "I need to move some furniture - could you help me or connect me with someone who could?"

Emotional support:

- "I need someone to check on me regularly because I tend to isolate when I'm struggling."
- "Could I call you when I'm having a hard time and just need someone to listen?"
- "I need friends who will include me in normal activities so I don't feel defined by my divorce."

- "I need people who can be patient with me while I figure out who I am as a single person."

Social support:

- "I'd love to be included in group activities, but I might need to bring my kids sometimes."
- "I need friends who won't treat me like I'm contagious because I'm divorced."
- "Could you invite me to things even if I might say no? I want to feel included even when I can't participate."

Spiritual support:

- "I'm struggling with my faith right now and could use prayer."
- "I need people who won't judge me for questioning God during this difficult time."
- "Could you help me find a church that's welcoming to divorced people?"

When People Respond Poorly

Not everyone will respond well to your honesty, and that's important information about those relationships. Some people will:

- Try to fix you or your marriage instead of supporting you
- Judge your decisions or offer unwanted advice
- Make it about them and their discomfort with divorce
- Disappear because they don't know how to handle difficult situations
- Take sides or try to get gossip about your ex

When this happens, it's disappointing but not surprising. Not everyone is equipped to walk through a crisis with you, and that's okay. Focus your energy on the people who respond with love and support, and don't waste time trying to convince others to care about you the way you need them to. You might be surprised by who steps up and who steps back. Sometimes people you thought were close friends disappear, and sometimes people you barely knew become your strongest supporters.

When you help others help you, you're not just getting the support you need - you're giving them a gift too. You're giving them:

The opportunity to make a difference. When you tell others specifically what you need, you give them a way to have a meaningful impact on your life.

A chance to practice love in action. It's easy to say you care about someone. It's harder to show up with dinner when they're too overwhelmed to cook. When you let people help you practically, you give them an opportunity to express their love tangibly.

Permission to be real about their own struggles. When you're honest about your difficulties, you often give others permission to be honest about theirs. Your vulnerability can deepen your relationships in unexpected ways.

A way to feel useful and needed. Helping others gives people a sense of purpose and contribution. When you let someone help you, you're allowing them to experience the joy of making a difference.

I recommend actually creating a visual map of your support network and being intentional about how you communicate with different circles of people:

Inner Circle (2-3 people): These are your ride-or-die people who get all the information and can handle your worst moments. They're on call for crisis situations. Jeff and I recommend if you do none of the other circles, at least give yourself this one.

Support Circle (5-10 people): These are close friends and family who get regular updates and can provide practical and emotional support. They know what's going on and how to help.

Community Circle (20-30 people): These are friends, neighbors, coworkers who know your basic situation and can provide occasional support. They might bring a meal or offer to help with kids.

Acquaintance Circle (everyone else): These people know you're going through a divorce but don't need details. They might offer general support or prayers.

Being intentional about these circles helps you:

- Share appropriate information with appropriate people
- Not overwhelm casual acquaintances with too much information
- Make sure your inner circle people don't get burned out
- Build a broad network of support rather than depending on just one or two people

Learning to be honest about your needs during divorce recovery is a skill that will serve you well for the rest of your life as Jeff and I have found out the hard way. Lots of these techniques and points we lay out in this book have come from what we wished we had done and had access to. We have learned that honest communication teaches you:

- How to identify what you actually need (which is harder than it sounds)
- How to communicate clearly and directly
- How to set appropriate boundaries
- How to build genuine, supportive relationships
- How to receive help gracefully
- How to discern who is trustworthy with your heart

These are life skills that will make all your future relationships healthier and more satisfying.

Scripture for Community Support:

"Two are better than one, because they have a good return for their labor: If either of them falls down, one can help the other up." - Ecclesiastes 4:9-10

"Therefore encourage one another and build each other up, just as in fact you are doing." - 1 Thessalonians 5:11

Chapter 10: Good Grief

The necessary work of mourning what's lost

"There is a time for everything, and a season for every activity under the heavens: a time to weep and a time to laugh, a time to mourn and a time to dance." - Ecclesiastes 3:1,4

This is a hard one, and so I'm not gonna sugarcoat it and pretend that it is not a hard one. But I want to let you know you're not alone, and you might even want to send this chapter to someone and say, "Okay, I've got to do this part. Help me."

This is about mourning. I'm sorry you have to do this, because I know how painful it was. That's why I hate to sit here and tell you, but it is necessary. We both realized - Jeff and I, going through divorces separately, we found both of us at some stage or other had to go through this point. And that's why we added it in here for you. There comes a point in time where you have to mourn everything you've lost.

I've been dreading writing this chapter. Not because I don't believe in what I'm going to tell you, but because I remember how much it hurt when I had to do this work myself. I remember the day I finally admitted to myself that I had to stop pretending some things weren't really gone and actually grieve them.

It was one of the hardest days of my recovery, and it was also one of the most important.

This chapter comes near the end of the Recovery Mode section because you need all the tools from the previous chapters to be able to handle this work. You need to have accepted your reality, honored your progress, built your support network, and learned to take care of yourself. Because mourning is intense work, and you need to be stable enough to do it without being destroyed by it.

But you can't fully move into Thriving Mode until you've done this work. You can't build a new life on top of ungrieved losses. You can't fully embrace your future until you've properly said goodbye to your past.

When you go through a divorce, you lose your significant other, you lose your partner, you lose your security. You might have lost financial things, you might have lost your home, you might have lost custody of children, you might have lost custody of animals. But you also lose everything that you had planned in your future - everything that could have been in that future is gone, and you have to mourn that.

Let me be specific about what you're actually grieving, because it's so much more than just the end of your marriage:

The person you thought your spouse was. Not necessarily who they actually were, but who you believed them to be. The version of them that you fell in love with, that you trusted, that you built dreams with.

The person you were in that relationship. The wife or husband version of yourself. The coupled version of yourself. The person who had a plus-one for everything, who made decisions as part of a team, who had someone to share daily life with.

The daily life you shared. Coming home and having someone to tell about your day. Having someone's schedule to coordinate with. Making dinner for two. Having someone to watch TV with at night. The mundane, ordinary moments that made life feel full.

The future you had planned. Retirement together. Growing old together. Traveling together. Grandchildren together. The house you were going to buy, the vacations you were going to take, the milestones you were going to celebrate together.

The dreams that will never be. The 25th anniversary you'll never have. The family traditions you'll never continue. The shared goals you'll never accomplish. The version of your family that will never exist.

The security and identity that came with being married. Feeling like you had life figured out. Having a clear role and identity. Feeling like you belonged somewhere, with someone. The sense of partnership and shared responsibility.

The innocence about love and marriage. The belief that love conquers all. The trust that marriage is permanent. The confidence that you can predict and control your future. The faith that doing the right things guarantees good outcomes.

All of this is real. All of this matters. All of this deserves to be grieved. Most of us resist the mourning process for several reasons:

It hurts too much. The pain of fully feeling your losses can be overwhelming. It's easier to stay busy, stay distracted, stay numb than to feel the full weight of what you've lost.

It feels ungrateful. You might think, "Other people have it worse. I should be grateful for what I still have, not mourning what I've lost."

It feels weak. Our culture tells us to be strong, to move on, to focus on the positive. Mourning can feel like wallowing or being stuck in the past.

It feels scary. You might be afraid that if you start grieving, you'll never stop. That the pain will swallow you whole and you'll never find your way back to joy.

But here's the truth: resistance to mourning is what keeps you stuck. You can't heal what you won't feel. You can't move forward while you're dragging unmourned losses behind you.

Let me be clear about something: there's a difference between healthy mourning and destructive wallowing.

Mourning is:

- Feeling your losses fully but with boundaries
- Processing grief with the intention of healing
- Acknowledging what's gone while remaining open to what's possible
- Crying, raging, or feeling sad with the support of others
- Moving through grief rather than setting up camp in it

Wallowing is:

- Getting stuck in grief without working through it
- Using grief as an excuse to avoid responsibility or growth
- Refusing comfort or support from others
- Making grief your identity rather than your process
- Staying in grief past the point where it's helpful

The goal of mourning is not to stay sad forever. The goal is to feel your losses completely so you can release them completely.

There are a lot of different ways that you can mourn something. It doesn't have to be long and drawn out. It doesn't have to be anything specific. It's whatever you - only you know how you mourn, and only you know what is therapeutic and helpful to you.

Some of these you may need and some you may not:

Writing and burning. Write out everything you're grieving - all your losses, all your disappointments, all your broken dreams. Then burn the papers in a safe place. The physical act of watching your words turn to ash can be very symbolic and healing.

Photo ritual. Go through photos from your marriage and really let yourself feel the memories. Don't just flip through quickly - sit with each picture and remember what life felt like then. Cry if you need to. Then put the photos away (don't throw them away, especially if you have children, but put them somewhere you won't see them regularly).

Letter writing. Write letters to your ex saying everything you never got to say. Write letters to your former self. Write letters to the dreams you're letting go of. You don't have to send these letters - they're for your healing, not for anyone else.

Memorial service. Have a private ceremony to honor what you've lost. Light candles, play meaningful music, speak out loud about what you're grieving. Some people do this alone, others invite close friends to witness their grief.

Physical release. Some people need to scream, punch pillows, go for intense runs, or find other physical ways to release the emotions. Grief isn't just emotional - it's stored in your body too.

Creative expression. Paint your grief. Write poetry about your losses. Create music that expresses what you can't say in words. Make something beautiful out of your pain.

Nature ritual. Go somewhere meaningful and spend time grieving outdoors. Some people throw stones in water, some bury symbolic objects, some just sit in nature and cry.

Talking it out. Tell a trusted friend or counselor about everything you're mourning. Sometimes we need to speak our losses out loud to someone who will witness our pain without trying to fix it.

For me, I'm a very action-oriented person. I gotta do something. I like writing stuff out and burning it. I took a journal that I had kept up until that time and I burned it. It was a very real raw emotional experience - like I wrote everything I really felt and thought.

I also had to go through a photo album and go through the memories. But those memories also triggered the future that I thought I was gonna have and the future hopes and dreams. So I had to really just have a crappy day, a crappy afternoon, kind of mourning it and being honest about it and being truthful to myself about how I felt.

I remember the day I decided to do this work. I had been avoiding it for months. I kept telling myself I was "being strong" and "focusing on the future." But I realized I wasn't actually moving forward - I was just staying busy to avoid feeling.

So I set aside a whole Saturday. I told my closest friend what I was planning to do and asked her to check on me that evening. I got out all the photo albums, all the keepsakes, all the mementos from our marriage. I made a cup of tea, put on music that meant something to us, and I let myself remember.

I looked at our wedding photos and mourned the bride who thought she was marrying her forever person. I looked at vacation pictures and mourned all the trips we'd never take. I looked at photos of us with friends and mourned the coupled social life I'd never have again. I looked at pictures of our house and mourned the home we'd built together.

And then I wrote. I wrote about every dream that was dying. I wrote about every plan that would never happen. I wrote about every future holiday, anniversary, and milestone that would look different now. I wrote about the grandparents we'd never be together, the retirement we'd never share, the old age we'd never experience side by side.

It was devastating. It was also necessary.

When I was done writing, I took all those pages outside and burned them. I watched the smoke carry my words up into the sky, and I felt something shift inside me. Not healing exactly - that would take much longer. But release. Permission to let go.

Here's why this painful process is so important: you cannot fully embrace your new life while you're still clinging to your old one. You cannot plant new dreams in soil that's still occupied by the roots of dead dreams.

Mourning creates space. It clears out the emotional clutter so you have room for new experiences, new relationships, new hopes, new joys.

Mourning honors what was real and meaningful in your past while freeing you to create meaning in your future.

Mourning allows you to love again - both yourself and others - without the weight of unprocessed loss making everything heavy.

After I did my mourning ritual, I noticed several changes:

- I felt lighter, like I'd been carrying a heavy backpack and finally set it down
- I had energy for new things instead of spending it all on holding onto old things
- I could think about my past without being overwhelmed
- I started feeling curious about my future instead of just afraid of it

Sometimes mourning includes anger, and that's okay. You might be angry at:

- Your ex for ending the marriage or for their choices that led to the end
- Yourself for not seeing warning signs or for your own mistakes
- God for allowing this to happen
- Life for not working out the way you planned
- Other people for having what you lost

Anger is often grief wearing a different costume. It's the emotion we feel when we're not ready to feel sad yet. Let yourself feel angry if that's what comes up, but don't get stuck there. Anger can be part of mourning, but it can't be the end point. If you find yourself stuck in anger for a long time, you might need professional help to work through it. Remember, we're not licensed counselors - we're just sharing what worked for us in our own experiences.

As Christians, mourning can bring up complex feelings about God's role in our loss. You might find yourself asking:

- Why did God allow this to happen?
- Is my divorce outside of God's will?
- How can I mourn something that might be sinful?
- Where is God's comfort when I need it most?

These are valid questions, and it's okay to wrestle with them. In fact, mourning often deepens our relationship with God because it forces us to be honest about our pain and our need for comfort that only He can provide. Some people find it helpful to think of mourning as a form of prayer - bringing our deepest pain to God and trusting Him with our broken hearts.

The psalms are full of mourning and lament. David regularly brought his grief, his anger, his confusion to God. We can do the same.

The mourning process doesn't happen once and then you're done forever. You might need to mourn different losses at different times. You might find yourself grieving again around anniversaries, holidays, or major life events.

But once you've done the deep work of mourning your primary losses, you'll notice:

- You can think about your past without being overwhelmed
- You have emotional energy available for new experiences
- You're curious about your future instead of just afraid of it
- You can support others going through similar losses
- You feel like yourself again, even though you're different than before

The goal isn't to never feel sad about your losses again. The goal is to feel sad when it's appropriate without being controlled by that sadness. You can do this. You're strong enough now to handle this work. You've survived everything else that divorce has thrown at you - you can survive mourning too.

And on the other side of mourning is freedom. Freedom to love again, to dream again, to hope again. Freedom to build a life that's not haunted by unprocessed loss. You don't have to do this work alone. Reach out to friends, family, counselors, or your faith community for support. Let people walk through this valley with you.

But don't skip this work because it's hard. Your future self - the thriving version of you that's waiting on the other side of this grief - is depending on you to do this hard thing now.

Scripture for Mourning:

"He heals the brokenhearted and binds up their wounds." - Psalm 147:3

"Weeping may stay for the night, but rejoicing comes in the morning." - Psalm 30:5

"Blessed are those who mourn, for they will be comforted." - Matthew 5:4

END OF PART TWO: RECOVERY MODE

Look at you. You've embraced your new reality, honored how far you've come, learned to let people help you, and done the hard work of mourning. This is recovery work, and it's some of the hardest emotional labor you'll ever do.

You should be proud of yourself. Not everyone has the courage to do this deep work. Many people get stuck in survival mode forever because they're afraid to face their new reality. But you did it. You looked your losses in the eye and grieved them properly.

Now, before you think about thriving, you need to know something: recovery isn't linear. You might have days where you feel like you're back in survival mode, and that's normal. Healing happens in waves, not straight lines.

You're ready for the thriving section when you can think about your future with hope instead of just fear. When you can see possibilities instead of just problems. When you can imagine good things ahead instead of just more loss.

But if you're not there yet, please don't force it. There's no shame in needing more time in recovery. Some of these chapters might need to be revisited multiple times. Some of this work might take years, not months. Let it take the time it takes.

Your healing is not a race. It's a journey, and you're exactly where you need to be.

Part Three: Thriving

BEGINNING OF PART THREE: THRIVING MODE

Friend, if you're reading this section, something has shifted in you. The crisis has passed. You've done the hard work of accepting your new reality and mourning your losses. You're not just surviving anymore - you're ready to start building something beautiful with the life you have now.

Thriving doesn't mean you never have bad days. It doesn't mean you're completely "over" your divorce. It means you can see good in your current life and hope for your future. It means you're ready to dream again, to forgive deeply, to find joy in unexpected places.

This section is about more than just getting back to where you were before. This is about becoming someone new - someone who has been through fire and come out stronger, someone who knows their own resilience, someone who can help others because they've walked this path.

Take your time here too. Some of these chapters will challenge you in new ways. But you're ready for this challenge because you've proven to yourself that you can survive anything.

Let's learn to thrive together.

Chapter 11: Shame and Forgiveness

Breaking free from what holds you back

---

*"There is now no condemnation for those who are in Christ Jesus." -
Romans 8:1*

We are into the section all about thriving, we want you to know that it
is possible to thrive during your divorce. We want to applaud you –
you are here. I promise you it does get better.

As Christians, we want to tell you that we have prayed over this book,
we've prayed over you, and we hope that you find this helpful and that
it encourages and just really comes alongside you and makes you
understand and know that the body of Christ is with you and you are
not alone.

I know right away you're like, "I don't want to hear this, I don't want to
deal with it," but hear me out. Hear us out. We think this is a
necessary step, not to forgive your ex or forgive your spouse and
have this big coming-back-together where everyone gets along
harmoniously. No. This is about shame and forgiveness – overcoming
it within yourself, for yourself, for your future growth, for if there's
children involved, for their future growth as well.

We felt, as Christians growing up in the faith and finding ourselves in
a divorce, we felt a lot of shame. It was just really difficult to even let
people know that I was going through a divorce, and him the same
way. It was hard to go to the bookstore and look for books on the
word "divorce." It was just a lot of shame.

As long as that shame is there, it keeps you from seeking the help
that you need, and it just keeps you from moving forward.

Let me tell you something about shame that I wish someone had told me earlier: shame is different from guilt, and understanding that difference can change everything. Guilt says, "I did something bad." Shame says, "I am something bad." Guilt is about actions. Shame is about identity. Guilt can be healthy – it helps us recognize when we've done something wrong and motivates us to make changes. But shame is never healthy. Shame tells us we are fundamentally flawed, unworthy of love, beyond redemption.

When you're carrying shame about your divorce, you're not just feeling bad about what happened. You're feeling bad about who you are. You're telling yourself stories like "I'm a failure as a wife/husband," or "I'm damaged goods," or "I'm not worthy of love," or "I'm a bad Christian," or "I'm a disappointment to God and everyone else." These shame messages keep you stuck. They keep you small. They keep you from believing you deserve good things or that God can still use your life in beautiful ways.

Shame around divorce can come from many sources. Sometimes it comes from church culture – some churches, intentionally or not, create environments where divorced people feel like second-class citizens, where married couples are held up as the gold standard and single people feel like they're missing something essential. Family expectations can also pile on shame, especially if you grew up in a family where divorce was unthinkable, where staying married no matter what was seen as the ultimate virtue.

Personal expectations can be just as damaging. Maybe you always thought you'd be the person who figured out how to make marriage work, who would never end up divorced like "those other people." Then there are societal messages – we live in a culture that often treats divorce as failure, as something shameful, as evidence that you couldn't handle adult responsibilities. And religious teachings can add another layer when you've been taught that God hates divorce so much that He must hate divorced people too.

All of these sources can pile shame on top of shame until you feel crushed under the weight of it. Here's the thing about shame: it becomes a prison that keeps you from the very things that could help you heal. Shame keeps you from reaching out for help because you don't want people to know how "badly" you've failed. It keeps you from believing you deserve good things in the future, from taking risks on new relationships because you're convinced you'll just mess them up too, from pursuing dreams and goals because you feel like you don't deserve success.

Shame prevents you from accepting love and support because you're convinced people would reject you if they really knew you. It stops you from trusting yourself to make good decisions because you're convinced you can't be trusted. Most devastatingly, shame keeps you from believing God still has good plans for your life. Shame is like wearing dark sunglasses that make everything look dim and hopeless. It distorts your vision of yourself, your future, and even God's heart toward you.

I carried enormous shame about my divorce for a long time. Even though I had what many people would consider biblical grounds for divorce, even though staying in my marriage had become emotionally and spiritually destructive, I still felt like a complete failure.

I felt ashamed when I walked into church. I felt ashamed when I had to check "divorced" on forms. I felt ashamed when people asked about my ex-husband. I felt ashamed when my children had to explain why Dad didn't live with us anymore. The shame was exhausting. It colored everything. It made me second-guess every decision, doubt every feeling, question every hope for the future.

One of the good ways of dealing with the shame — honestly, one of the good ways of dealing with all the different emotions, anger and fear, all of those — is to journal. Journaling may not work for you. I never journaled until I went through a divorce, and then I was journaling every single day.

Jeff does not journal and he never did journal through it, but he still found ways to work on solitary projects where he could kind of think and process things.

But for me it was journaling, and so you need to express it in whatever way helps you to get all that shame out. The shame is not doing anything but holding you back.

There's a difference between shame and guilt and conviction, and I'm not talking about your former spouse, your ex – this is about you. This is how you feel and how you're going forward.

Conviction comes from the Holy Spirit and leads to repentance and restoration. It says, "You did something that hurt yourself or others, and God wants to help you change." Conviction is specific, hopeful, and leads to growth. Shame comes from the enemy and leads to despair and isolation. It says, "You are fundamentally flawed and unworthy of love." Shame is vague, hopeless, and leads to hiding.

When God convicts us of sin, He also provides the path to forgiveness and healing. When shame attacks us, it just tears us down without offering any hope for redemption. If you're feeling convicted about specific things you did wrong during your marriage or divorce, that's actually good news. It means God is still working in your life, still wanting to help you grow and change. But if you're feeling generally worthless and unlovable because of your divorce, that's shame, and it's not from God.

My biggest advice is give it to Christ, give it to God. He already knows how you feel, he knows the shame that you feel. I'm talking whether you were the offender or the offended, whether you did nothing and you were always the good – not the good, but the spouse that gave the other spouse everything they needed and you never did anything wrong. In other words, you're perfect.

But most all of us are flawed individuals, and at some point, somewhere, some way, we've done something to offend someone else. So you just give all that to God, give that shame to Him. Here's what I had to learn: God can handle my shame. He's not shocked by it, overwhelmed by it, or disgusted by it. He's seen it all before, and He loves me anyway.

When I finally brought my shame to God – really brought it, not just mentioned it in passing during prayer but really laid it all out – something amazing happened. I felt His love for me in a way I never had before. Not His love for the perfect version of me, but His love for the real, flawed, divorced, struggling me.

God doesn't love us in spite of our brokenness – He loves us right in the middle of it. He doesn't wait for us to clean ourselves up before He extends His grace. He meets us in our mess and loves us there.

Forgiveness. I know how people feel about forgiveness, but I'm just going to tell you the truth, my truth, and Jeff's truth. Forgiveness is about you and for you. It is not for the other person.

I'm not talking about you forgive them and now y'all are best friends and they come around all the time. If that can happen in your relationship, wonderful. But for most people, it's within ourselves we just forgive, we let it go. We don't even – you're not even trying to seek to understand why, what happened, where it happened, when. It's just "I let it go."

I forgive myself for my flaws, for my part in the downfall of that marriage, and I forgive the other person because I need to, because I need to move on, because I no longer need to allow them to hold space within me that's negative, that will eat me alive. That's why we do it, and that's why when you can do this step, you're starting to really truly thrive and recover, truly recover from your divorce.

Let me be really clear about what forgiveness is and isn't. Forgiveness is a choice, not a feeling. It's for your benefit, not necessarily theirs. It's letting go of your right to revenge and releasing the other person from the debt they owe you. It's freeing yourself from the prison of bitterness and it's a process, not a one-time event. But forgiveness is not excusing what they did or pretending it didn't hurt. It's not trusting them again automatically or welcoming them back into your life. It's not forgetting what happened or being friends with them.

You can forgive someone and still maintain boundaries. You can forgive someone and still protect yourself from future harm. You can forgive someone and still acknowledge that what they did was wrong.

I have found that the hardest person to forgive is yourself. You might be carrying guilt and shame about things you said or did during the marriage, ways you contributed to the problems, mistakes you made during the divorce process, choices that hurt your children, or times you weren't the person you wanted to be.

Self-forgiveness is crucial because you cannot build a healthy future while constantly punishing yourself for the past.

Forgiving yourself doesn't mean excusing your mistakes, pretending you didn't do anything wrong, or avoiding responsibility for your actions. Forgiving yourself means acknowledging your mistakes without being defined by them, learning from your failures without being destroyed by them, accepting that you did the best you could with what you knew at the time, believing that you're worthy of grace and second chances, and choosing to treat yourself with the same compassion you'd show a friend.

Forgiving your ex-spouse might be the hardest forgiveness work you'll ever do, especially if they had an affair, abandoned the family, were abusive, fought dirty during the divorce, or continue to make your life difficult.

Here's what I learned about forgiving my ex: I didn't forgive him because he deserved it. I forgave him because I deserved to be free from the bitterness that was eating me alive. Carrying unforgiveness is like drinking poison and expecting the other person to get sick. It doesn't hurt them — it hurts you. It keeps you emotionally tied to someone you're trying to move on from. Forgiveness doesn't mean what they did was okay. It means you're not going to let what they did continue to control your life.

Forgiveness isn't usually a one-time decision — it's a process that happens over time. Here's what that process might look like.

First, you acknowledge the hurt. You can't forgive what you won't admit hurt you. Be honest about the damage that was done. Then you feel your feelings. Anger, sadness, betrayal — feel it all. You can't forgive from a place of denial. Next, you choose to forgive. This is a decision of your will, not your emotions. You might not feel forgiving yet, but you can choose to move in that direction.

Then you release the debt. Stop demanding that they pay for what they did. Stop rehearsing their crimes in your mind. Stop waiting for them to grovel or apologize. If you can, pray for them. This might seem impossible at first, but praying for someone who hurt you can help your heart soften toward them. And then you repeat as necessary. You might have to choose forgiveness multiple times as new hurts surface or old wounds get triggered.

Sometimes forgiveness feels completely impossible. The hurt is too deep, the betrayal too severe, the ongoing damage too real. If that's where you are, start smaller. Ask God to help you want to forgive. Pray for willingness to be willing. Focus on forgiving one specific incident rather than everything at once. Work with a counselor who can help you process the deeper wounds. Remember that forgiveness is a journey, not a destination.

You don't have to rush forgiveness. You don't have to pretend you're further along than you are. But don't give up on it either, because forgiveness is one of the keys to your freedom.

When you truly forgive – both yourself and others – something shifts inside you. You'll notice mental freedom where you stop obsessing about what happened, replaying conversations, planning what you wish you'd said. You'll experience emotional freedom where you're not constantly angry, bitter, or hurt, and you have emotional energy available for positive things.

There's spiritual freedom where your relationship with God deepens because you're not carrying the weight of unforgiveness between you. You'll find relational freedom where you can build new relationships without the baggage of past hurts contaminating them. You'll even notice physical freedom because bitterness and unforgiveness actually affect your physical health – forgiveness can literally make you feel better. Most importantly, you'll experience future freedom where you can dream and plan and hope again because you're not stuck in the past.

One of the biggest misconceptions about forgiveness is that it means you have to let people back into your life or trust them again. That's not true. Forgiveness is about your heart. Boundaries are about your safety and wisdom.

You can forgive someone and still refuse to be alone with them, limit your communication to what's necessary, protect your children from their destructive behavior, keep them from knowing personal details about your life, and say no to their requests for help or favors. Forgiveness opens your heart. Boundaries protect your life. You need both.

My friend, you can do it. It is all an act within yourself, a just taking time, taking a deep breath, journaling, breathing it through, and saying, asking yourself, "Do I feel shameful? If I do, okay, I'm gonna let that go. I'm gonna let that shame just go. Do I feel any more unforgiveness? Am I holding on to this? Okay, I'm just gonna let it go. For me, for my children, for those around me, I'm gonna let this go so that I can grow and truly thrive in my new life."

You deserve to be free from shame. You deserve to be free from bitterness. You deserve to build a beautiful future that's not haunted by an unforgiving past. The shame you're carrying? It's not from God. The unforgiveness you're holding? It's not protecting you. They're both prisons that are keeping you from the abundant life God wants for you.

Today, choose freedom. Choose forgiveness. Choose to believe that your best days are ahead of you, not behind you.

You've got this.

Prayers for Forgiveness:

"God, I choose to forgive [name] for [specific hurt]. I release them from the debt they owe me and ask You to heal my heart."

"Lord, help me forgive myself for [specific mistake]. I accept Your grace and choose to treat myself with compassion."

"Father, I give You my shame about my divorce. Replace it with Your truth about who I am in Christ."

Scripture for Forgiveness:

"Be kind and compassionate to one another, forgiving each other, just as in Christ God forgave you." - Ephesians 4:32

"If we confess our sins, he is faithful and just and will forgive us our sins and purify us from all unrighteousness." - 1 John 1:9

"Bear with each other and forgive one another if any of you has a grievance against someone. Forgive as the Lord forgave you." - Colossians 3:13

Chapter 12: Let It Go!

Removing reminders while honoring the past

"Forget the former things; do not dwell on the past. See, I am doing a new thing! Now it springs up; do you not perceive it?" - Isaiah 43:18-19

Jeff and I, both realized it came to the point where we needed to get things out of our eyesight, out of our home and out of our car that belonged to our ex-spouse, or reminded us of our past relationship.

With that, I'm not saying go toss it out the door, go put it in a trash bag and get rid of it and toss it away. There might be some things that you can do that with. However, if you have children, I think it's extremely important that you honor your past relationship.

Let me tell you something about living with constant reminders of your former marriage: it's like trying to heal a wound while someone keeps picking at the scab.

Every photo on the refrigerator. Every piece of furniture you bought together. Every coffee mug that was his favorite. Every book she left on the nightstand. Every Christmas ornament that represents a trip you took together. Every single thing becomes a tiny emotional assault throughout your day.

You wake up and see the wedding photo still hanging in the hallway. You make coffee with the mug he brought you from that business trip. You sit in the chair where she used to read every evening. You go to bed looking at the dresser that still has her jewelry box on it.

These aren't necessarily bad memories. Sometimes the good memories are harder to live with than the bad ones. The bad memories make you angry, which gives you energy. The good memories make you sad, which depletes your energy.

When you're in Thriving Mode, you're ready to create space for new memories, new traditions, new life. But you can't do that when every corner of your home is a shrine to what used to be.

One part of thriving is to put things away and get them out of your sight, but in an honorable way. You know, there's a way to hold on to things so if you had children - I really can't say this enough - it is your responsibility to hold on to that for them. That's their legacy, that's their history, and I don't think it's right in any way - and I don't care if you are the major offender of the relationship or the major wounded one - you don't have the right, in my opinion, to just toss out your kids' legacy.

I say let it go, get it out of your sight. That is healthy and good. Yes, if it evokes - every time you walk through a room you see that picture or you see that thing that you bought on a trip somewhere - then yes, I say remove it, get it out. But pack it away, put it up, and put it away somewhere so that you have it there for your family, for your children, for those that that relationship is part of their legacy, part of their history. You need to honor that.

Let me be very clear about what I mean by "letting go":

Letting go means:

- Removing items from your daily environment that trigger painful memories
- Storing meaningful items safely for potential future use
- Creating space for new memories and experiences
- Choosing not to be surrounded by constant reminders of your past
- Making your home feel like YOUR space, not a museum of your marriage

Letting go does NOT mean:

- Destroying everything from your marriage
- Pretending your marriage never happened
- Removing all evidence of your children's family history
- Acting like your ex-spouse never existed
- Throwing away items that might have future value or meaning

What Needs to Go (And Where It Should Go)

Different items require different approaches. Here's how I think about various categories:

Daily use items that trigger memories:

- His coffee mug → donate or give to him
- Her favorite blanket → store in attic or give to her
- Shared towels and linens → replace with new ones that are just yours
- Kitchen gadgets that remind you of cooking together → store or donate

Sentimental items with family value:

- Wedding photos → carefully stored for children's future use
- Family vacation photos → kept but moved from public display to storage
- Gifts between spouses → stored for potential future appreciation
- Items from shared experiences → packed away with care

Furniture and large items:

- Bedroom furniture → replace if possible, especially the bed
- Shared furniture → keep what you love, replace what triggers memories
- His recliner → offer to him or donate
- Items that dominate the space → consider whether they fit your new life

Children's items related to family:

- Photos of family together → absolutely keep, even if stored temporarily
- Gifts from the other parent → keep for children
- Family heirlooms → preserve for next generation
- Memory books or scrapbooks → store safely for when children are older

When I was ready to do this work, I realized that almost everything in my house told the story of "us." The couch we picked out together. The dishes we got for our wedding. The artwork we bought on our honeymoon. The Christmas decorations we'd collected over the years.

I couldn't throw it all away - some of it was expensive, some had sentimental value for the kids, and some of it I actually still liked. But I also couldn't live in a shrine to my failed marriage.

So I developed a system:

Keep and enjoy: Items I loved that didn't trigger painful memories
Store for later: Items with family value that I wasn't ready to see daily
Give to him: Items that were clearly his or that he might want
Donate: Items that neither of us wanted but were still useful **Replace gradually:** Items I used daily that triggered memories

The process took months. I didn't do it all at once because that would have been overwhelming and expensive. I did it gradually, replacing and rearranging as I could afford to and as I felt emotionally ready.

The Bedroom: Your Most Important Space

If there's one room that absolutely must be transformed, it's your bedroom. This is where you begin and end each day. This is your most private, personal space. This cannot remain a memorial to your marriage.

You don't have to replace everything, but you need to make it feel like YOUR space:

The bed: If at all possible, get a new mattress. If you can't afford new, at least get new bedding - sheets, comforters, pillows. Nothing says "new life" like a bed that's completely yours.

Photos: Remove all photos of you as a couple from the bedroom. You can store them, but you shouldn't fall asleep and wake up looking at images of your former life.

Personal items: Remove his cologne, her jewelry, shared books, anything that makes it feel like they might come back.

Décor: Change something about the look of the room. Paint a wall, rearrange the furniture, add new curtains. Make it reflect who you are now, not who you were then.

Scent: This might sound silly, but scent is powerfully connected to memory. If the room smells like your former life, change that. New candles, new air freshener, new laundry detergent.

The Kitchen: Creating New Routines

The kitchen can be especially triggering because it's where so much of daily family life happened. You cooked his favorite meals. You sat at that table for thousands of conversations. You opened birthday presents and helped with homework and had family meetings.

But the kitchen is also where you can most powerfully create new life:

Cooking for one: Learn to cook meals you actually want to eat, not just what the family would eat **New dishes:** If you can afford it, get some new plates, cups, utensils that are just yours **Rearrange:** Change where things go so you're not automatically reaching for "his" mug or "her" favorite pan **New routines:** Create new traditions around meals, even if it's just eating breakfast on the porch instead of at the table

Photos: The Most Difficult Decision

Photos are probably the hardest items to deal with because they're so emotionally charged. Here's my approach:

Wedding photos: Store these carefully. Your children may want them someday, even if you never want to see them again.

Family photos: Keep all photos that include your children. Store them if you can't look at them now, but preserve them for your kids.

Couple photos: Store these too. You might never want them, but your children might appreciate having pictures of their parents together.

Daily display: Create new photo displays that reflect your current life. Photos of you with friends, you with your children, your children alone, your extended family.

The goal isn't to pretend your marriage never happened - it's to stop living in visual reminders of it every day.

What About Gifts?

Gifts between spouses are particularly complicated:

- Jewelry he gave you
- Tools she bought for your hobby
- Books you gave each other
- Art you selected together

My rule of thumb: if you genuinely love the item and it doesn't trigger painful memories, keep it. If it was expensive and practical, keep it. If looking at it makes you sad or angry, store it or give it away.

Your engagement ring and wedding ring deserve special consideration. Some people keep them for their children. Some people sell them and use the money for something meaningful. Some people have them redesigned into new jewelry. Do what feels right for you, but don't feel obligated to keep wearing them or displaying them.

Digital Reminders

Don't forget about digital reminders:

- Photos on your phone and computer
- Social media posts and pictures
- Shared online accounts
- Digital music playlists that remind you of your marriage

You don't have to delete everything, but you might want to:

- Create new folders for old photos so you don't see them accidentally
- Unlink shared accounts
- Create new playlists with music for your new life
- Update your screensavers and profile pictures

If you had no children and you think your children don't want any of this, you know there's no one in your family that wants this stuff, I say because you're moving into thriving, put it into a box still, put the stuff away and don't toss it just put it away. Because at this point, you're just honoring yourself and your truth, and I think it's still too emotionally involved. And what's the harm? What is the harm of putting it up, putting it away and not tossing it right now? There is no harm.

There might be some things that you need to get out because they're large - like a recliner or chair, things like that. Of course you could do that. And always ask the other person, "Do you want this?" You know, maybe they want it.

But I think today's "letting it go" is therapeutic, it is a really good process and step. But just remember: let it go, but meaning out of your immediate sphere, out of your immediate space. Be careful to not just toss things away.

This is important because:

- You might feel differently about items in the future
- You might discover things have more value than you realized
- Your children might want things when they're older that they don't want now
- You're making decisions from an emotional place, which isn't always the best place for permanent choices

The real purpose of letting go isn't just to remove painful reminders - it's to create space for new life to grow. When you remove the photos of your old life, you create wall space for art that reflects who you're becoming. When you pack away the dishes you got for your wedding, you create room for dishes that you choose for yourself. When you move the furniture that dominated your living room, you create space to arrange things in a way that makes you happy.

Every item you let go of creates space for something new to enter your life.

The Emotional Process

Don't be surprised if this work brings up a lot of emotions. You might feel:

- Sadness about the good memories
- Anger about the waste of money and time

- Relief about finally making your space your own
- Guilt about "erasing" your marriage
- Fear about truly moving forward
- Excitement about creating something new

All of these feelings are normal. Let yourself feel them, but don't let them stop you from doing the work.

When It's Done

You'll know you've done enough of this work when:

- Your home feels like YOUR home, not a shared space
- You can move through your daily routines without constant memory triggers
- Your space reflects who you are now, not who you used to be
- You feel peaceful and comfortable in your environment
- You're excited about creating new memories in your space

This doesn't mean your home has to be completely free of any reminders of your past. It means the reminders that remain are ones you've consciously chosen to keep, not ones you're keeping out of habit, obligation, or inability to make decisions.

Letting go of physical reminders is really about giving yourself permission to start fresh. It's about creating an environment that supports your new life instead of constantly reminding you of your old one. You're not erasing your history - you're choosing not to live in it. You're not dishonoring your past - you're making room for your future. You're not being disrespectful to your ex or your children - you're being respectful to yourself and your need to heal and move forward.

This is therapeutic work. This is a really good process and step. But remember: let it go out of your immediate sphere, out of your immediate space, but be careful not to just toss things away. Honor your past by preserving what matters. Honor your future by creating space for it to unfold.

Scripture for New Beginnings:

"See, I am doing a new thing! Now it springs up; do you not perceive it? I am making a way in the wilderness and streams in the wasteland." - Isaiah 43:19

"Therefore, if anyone is in Christ, the new creation has come: The old has gone, the new is here!" - 2 Corinthians 5:17

Chapter 13: Time to Dream Again

Beginning to plan and hope for the future

"'For I know the plans I have for you,' declares the Lord, 'plans to prosper you and not to harm you, to give you hope and a future.'" - Jeremiah 29:11

It's time for you to start planning a new life. I had a life track in my previous marriage, and I even had it planned for our retirement. We had the dream that we were going to drive around the country in an RV. So those were things that I had planned within that marriage, with that person that I had to do the whole letting go of and mourning all of it.

But then there comes a point in time, which we are at now, which is when you need to start dreaming again. You need to start creating new plans for yourself, and that can be the same plans but maybe it looks a little bit differently. Or it could be, "You know what, I'm going to embrace a whole new attitude, and maybe I'm gonna fly or start taking cruises," or you know, anything.

It's just time for you to start planning and beginning again so that you can start thriving during this time. If you're reading this chapter and feeling scared, overwhelmed, or even resistant to the idea of dreaming again, that's completely normal. Dreaming again after divorce can feel terrifying for so many reasons:

Fear of disappointment: "What if I dream again and it all falls apart like my marriage did?"

Fear of betrayal: "Is it disloyal to my old dreams to dream new ones?"

Fear of judgment: "What will people think if I start hoping for things again so soon?"

Fear of vulnerability: "What if I put myself out there and get hurt again?"

Fear of failure: "What if I'm not capable of building a good life on my own?"

Fear of the unknown: "I don't even know who I am anymore, how can I know what I want?"

Let me tell you something: all of these fears are normal, and none of them are reasons to stop dreaming. Fear is not a reliable compass for life decisions. Fear wants to keep you small, safe, and stuck. Dreams require courage, but they also create hope.

The dreams you had in your marriage were beautiful and meaningful, and it's okay to grieve them. You had plans, goals, visions of your future that included another person. You saw yourself growing old with someone, sharing grandchildren, traveling together, building a life side by side.

Those dreams mattered. They were real. They were good dreams. But they're gone now, and you have a choice: you can spend the rest of your life mourning what will never be, or you can invest your energy in dreaming what could be.

New dreams aren't replacements for old dreams - they're completely different dreams for a completely different life. You're not the same person you were when you got married. You've been through things, learned things, survived things that have changed you. The person you are now might want different things than the person you were then. And that's not just okay - that's beautiful.

I remember the first time someone asked me what I wanted for my future after my divorce. I literally couldn't answer. I had spent so many years thinking in terms of "we" that I had no idea what "I" wanted.

"What kind of house do you want to live in?" "What do you want to do for work?" "Where do you want to travel?" "What do you want your life to look like in five years?"

I realized I hadn't thought about my individual desires in so long that I'd forgotten I had any. My dreams had become so intertwined with my marriage that I couldn't separate what I wanted from what we had wanted together.

So I started small. I started with tiny dreams:

- I want to paint my bedroom a color I love
- I want to try a restaurant I've never been to
- I want to read books that interest me
- I want to listen to music that makes me happy

From those tiny dreams, bigger dreams started to emerge:

- I want to travel to places I've always been curious about
- I want to pursue interests I put aside during my marriage
- I want to build friendships with people who really know me
- I want to create a home that reflects my personality
- I want to do work that feels meaningful to me

And eventually, even bigger dreams:

- I want to love and be loved again
- I want to build a life that's authentically mine
- I want to use my experience to help other people
- I want to discover what I'm capable of when I'm not holding myself back

When you're starting to dream again, it helps to think in different categories:

Immediate dreams (next 6 months):

- How do you want your daily life to feel?
- What changes do you want to make to your living space?
- What new routines or habits do you want to establish?
- What relationships do you want to invest in?

Short-term dreams (1-2 years):

- Do you want to change jobs or careers?
- Do you want to move to a different place?
- What skills or education do you want to pursue?
- What experiences do you want to have?

Medium-term dreams (3-5 years):

- What kind of lifestyle do you want to build?
- Do you want to date again? Remarry?
- Do you want to have more children?
- What financial goals do you want to achieve?

Long-term dreams (5+ years):

- How do you want to spend your retirement?
- What legacy do you want to leave?
- What would you regret not doing if you looked back from age 80?
- What impact do you want to have on the world?

Relationship dreams:

- Do you want to date again?
- What qualities would you want in a future partner?
- Do you want to remarry someday?
- What would a healthy relationship look like for you now?

Family dreams:

- Do you want more children?
- How do you want to co-parent with your ex?
- What traditions do you want to create with your kids?
- How do you want your family structure to evolve?

Career dreams:

- Do you want to change fields completely?
- Do you want to go back to school?
- Do you want to start your own business?
- What kind of work would feel meaningful to you?

Adventure dreams:

- Where do you want to travel?
- What experiences do you want to have?
- What have you always wanted to try?
- What would push you outside your comfort zone in a good way?

I love vision boards and buying a new journal, and there's real power in writing down your dreams. When dreams live only in your head, they can feel vague and impossible. When you write them down, they become more concrete and achievable.

Start with brain-dumping everything you might want, without editing or judging:

- I might want to learn Spanish
- I might want to move to a smaller town
- I might want to get a dog
- I might want to take art classes
- I might want to date someone who loves hiking
- I might want to visit Ireland
- I might want to write a book
- I might want to learn to cook for one person

Don't worry about whether these dreams are practical, affordable, or realistic right now. Just get them out of your head and onto paper.

Then start organizing them:

- Which dreams excite you most?
- Which dreams feel achievable in the next year?
- Which dreams would require major life changes?
- Which dreams align with your values and priorities?
- Which dreams feel like they come from fear vs. genuine desire?

There's a difference between dreams and plans, and both are important:

Dreams are about vision and possibility. They answer the question "What do I want my life to look like?" Dreams give you direction and motivation.

Plans are about strategy and action. They answer the question "How am I going to make this happen?" Plans give you concrete steps to take.

You need dreams to know where you're going, and you need plans to actually get there. Some of your dreams might need to stay dreams for now - and that's okay. Maybe you dream of traveling the world, but right now you need to focus on getting financially stable. Keep the dream alive, but make plans for the life you can actually build right now.

Other dreams might be ready to become plans immediately. Maybe you've always wanted to take piano lessons. That's something you could potentially start next month if it's important to you.

One of the biggest barriers to dreaming again is getting overwhelmed by practical obstacles:

"I can't afford to travel." "I don't have time to go back to school." "I can't date because I have kids." "I can't move because of custody arrangements." "I can't change careers because I need stable income."

All of these obstacles might be real, but they're not necessarily permanent. And they're not reasons to stop dreaming entirely. Instead of letting obstacles kill your dreams, let them inform your timeline and strategy:

If money is tight: Focus on dreams that don't require a lot of money, or dreams that could potentially help you earn more money long-term.

If time is limited: Look for dreams you can pursue in small increments, or dreams that could actually simplify your life.

If you have children: Include them in age-appropriate dreams, or find dreams that make you a happier, more fulfilled parent.

If you have custody restrictions: Focus on dreams that work within your current situation, while keeping bigger dreams alive for the future.

If you need stability: Pursue dreams that add meaning to your life without adding chaos.

Remember: you don't have to achieve all your dreams immediately. You just need to start moving in the direction of the life you want to build.

Sometimes your new dreams might look surprisingly similar to your old dreams, just with different details. And that's perfectly okay. Jeff and I had a saying we developed while crafting this chapter. When Old become New Again. We realized that our old dreams ones way long ago forgotten, discarded, or even given up on could be resurrected again and become new again.

Maybe you still want to travel around the country, but now you're thinking about doing it solo or with friends instead of with a spouse. Maybe you still want to have a beautiful home, but now it's going to reflect your taste instead of compromise. Maybe you still want to grow old surrounded by family, but now that family might look different than you originally imagined.

You don't have to completely reinvent yourself to have new dreams. You might discover that some of your core desires remain the same - you just need to find new ways to pursue them. The best dreams are often the ones that scare you a little bit. Not the dreams that terrify you, but the dreams that make you think, "I don't know if I could actually do that, but wow, what if I could?"

Maybe it's starting your own business. Maybe it's moving to a different state. Maybe it's going back to school. Maybe it's learning a new skill. Maybe it's traveling somewhere alone. Maybe it's writing a book. Maybe it's running a marathon.

These dreams push you to grow. They require you to become more than you are right now. They keep life interesting and give you something to work toward. Pay attention to the dreams that make your heart race a little bit with possibility and fear. Those might be the most important ones to pursue.

Once you've identified some dreams, it's time to create a vision for your future. This might involve:

Vision boards: Cut out pictures and words that represent your dreams and arrange them on a board where you'll see them regularly.

Writing exercises: Write detailed descriptions of what your ideal day, week, or year would look like.

Goal setting: Choose specific dreams to focus on and break them down into actionable steps.

Timeline creation: Map out when you might pursue different dreams based on your current circumstances.

Accountability: Share your dreams with trusted friends who can encourage you and hold you accountable.

Starting Small

You don't have to pursue all your dreams at once. In fact, it's better to start small and build momentum.

Pick one dream that:

- Excites you
- Feels achievable in the near term
- Doesn't require major life upheaval
- Aligns with your current values and priorities

Focus on that one dream. Take concrete steps toward it. Achieve it. Let the success build your confidence for pursuing bigger dreams. Maybe it's as simple as redecorating your bedroom. Maybe it's taking a weekend trip somewhere you've never been. Maybe it's signing up for a class. Maybe it's joining a group or club. Small dreams achieved build the foundation for bigger dreams pursued.

This isn't about replacing your old life with an identical new life. This is about writing completely new chapters that you never could have imagined when you were married. Some of those chapters might be better than anything you experienced in your marriage. Some might be more challenging. All of them will be yours.

You get to decide what your story looks like from here. You get to choose what adventures to pursue, what goals to chase, what kind of person to become. Your story isn't over. In many ways, it's just beginning. So start dreaming. Start planning. Start believing that your best days are ahead of you, not behind you.

It's time to begin again.

Chapter 14: Find the Good

Celebrating what's working in your life now

"Give thanks in all circumstances; for this is God's will for you in Christ Jesus." - 1 Thessalonians 5:18

Divorce is a ripping apart. It is a shattering. It is the end of dreams, hopes, reality. It is a painful experience. So when you get to this part where you have just processed all of that and all of a sudden you can go, "You know what, there is good in my life right now" - that's when you know there's this little bud that has just popped up out of the ground. There's new life, there's new hope, and that's when you realize you're beginning to thrive.

If you've made it to this chapter, you've done incredibly hard work. You've survived the initial trauma. You've accepted your new reality. You've honored your progress. You've helped others help you. You've mourned your losses. You've worked on forgiveness. You've let go of physical reminders. You've started dreaming again.

And now? Now it's time to look around at the life you're actually living right now and find the good in it.

This isn't about pretending everything is perfect. This isn't about toxic positivity or minimizing your pain. This is about training your eyes to see what's working, what's beautiful, what's hopeful in your current circumstances.

Because here's the truth: there IS good in your life right now. It might be buried under stress and grief and exhaustion, but it's there. And learning to see it, acknowledge it, and yes, even celebrate it, is crucial for your continued healing and growth.

I think sometimes we can put on our negative glasses and all we see is the negative around us. And taking off those glasses and going, "Okay, I'm looking for something good that has come from this" - I promise you, something good has come from it.

When you're in the middle of trauma and crisis, your brain naturally focuses on threats, problems, and what's wrong. This is actually a survival mechanism - your brain is trying to keep you safe by constantly scanning for danger.

But what happens is that this threat-detection mode can become your default way of seeing the world. Even when you're no longer in immediate danger, even when things are starting to stabilize, your brain keeps looking for what's wrong instead of what's right.

Those "negative glasses" filter out the good things that are happening and magnify the problems. They make you feel like nothing is going well, like you're not making progress, like your life is just one disaster after another.

But that's not the whole truth. That's just the truth your traumatized brain is showing you. Taking off those glasses - consciously choosing to look for the good - isn't denial. It's balance. It's seeing your whole reality, not just the difficult parts.

The good in your life right now might not be dramatic or obvious. It might be quiet, subtle, easy to overlook. But it's there.

Environmental good: Maybe your home environment is less stressful now because there are no more arguments or tension. Maybe you can watch shows you couldn't watch before. Maybe you can go outside and watch the birds or take walks without having to consider someone else's schedule.

Relational good: Maybe you have more time to spend with your children, being present with them. Maybe you're building deeper friendships because you're more available. Maybe your relationship with God is closer because He truly is number one in your life now without having to compete with a spouse.

Personal good: Maybe this was a huge wake-up call and you're now taking better care of yourself physically, emotionally, or spiritually. Maybe you're discovering aspects of yourself that you'd forgotten or never knew existed.

Practical good: Maybe you have more control over your schedule, your finances, your daily decisions. Maybe you're learning skills you never had to learn before. Maybe you're becoming more independent and self-reliant.

Spiritual good: Maybe your faith is deeper and more authentic because it's been tested. Maybe you're experiencing God's comfort in ways you never have before. Maybe you're discovering that God's love for you isn't dependent on your circumstances.

Future good: Maybe you can see possibilities for your life that weren't there before. Maybe you have hope for things that couldn't happen while you were married. Maybe you're excited about opportunities that are opening up.

I'll be honest - for a long time after my divorce, I couldn't see any good. All I could see was what I'd lost, what had gone wrong, how hard everything was. I was wearing those negative glasses so tightly that they felt like part of my face.

But slowly, as I started to heal, little bits of good began to emerge:

I could paint my bedroom any color I wanted. This seems so small, but it was huge for me. For the first time in years, I could make a decision about my living space without having to compromise or negotiate.

I could eat dinner at 5:30 if I wanted to. Again, tiny, but it represented freedom. I could structure my day around what worked for me and my kids, not around someone else's preferences.

I rediscovered friendships that had taken a backseat during my marriage. I had more time and emotional energy to invest in relationships that nourished me.

I started sleeping better. Without the stress and tension of a troubled marriage, my body could actually rest.

I felt more like myself. I realized I had been trying to be someone else's version of a good wife for so long that I'd lost touch with who I actually was. Being single gave me space to rediscover my own personality, interests, and values.

My relationship with God deepened. When everything else felt unstable, I clung to God in a way I never had before. That desperation led to intimacy.

I became a better mother. When I wasn't pouring energy into a dysfunctional marriage, I had more to give to my children. And when I started taking better care of myself, I modeled self-respect for them.

I discovered I was stronger than I thought. Every challenge I navigated as a single person proved to me that I was capable of more than I'd believed.

None of these things happened overnight. And they didn't erase the pain of divorce or make everything easy. But they were real, significant improvements in my quality of life that came directly from my new circumstances.

Different Types of Good to Look For

Relief-based good: Things that are better because stress or conflict has been removed. You can breathe easier. You can relax in your own home. You don't have to walk on eggshells.

Discovery-based good: Things you're learning about yourself or experiencing for the first time. New interests, new strengths, new perspectives, new friendships.

Growth-based good: Ways you're becoming a better person because of what you've been through. More compassionate, more resilient, more authentic, more grateful.

Freedom-based good: Choices you can make now that you couldn't make before. Where to live, how to spend your time, what to prioritize, how to raise your children.

Relationship-based good: Connections that are deeper, healthier, or more possible because of your new situation. With your children, your friends, your family, or with God.

Future-based good: Possibilities that exist now that didn't exist before. New dreams, new opportunities, new directions your life could take.

Present-moment good: Simple pleasures and daily joys that you can notice and appreciate. A good cup of coffee, a beautiful sunset, a laugh with a friend, a hug from your child.

Finding the good isn't a one-time exercise - it's a practice that needs to be cultivated over time. Our brains are naturally wired to notice problems and threats, so noticing good things requires intentional effort.

Start a gratitude journal. Write down three things you're grateful for each day. They don't have to be big things. "I'm grateful for hot coffee this morning" counts.

Share good things with others. Tell a friend about something positive that happened in your day. Post something encouraging on social media. Share your gratitude in prayer.

Take photos of good moments. When you see something beautiful, experience something joyful, or notice something you're grateful for, take a picture. Create a photo album of good things from your new life.

Practice the "gratitude pause." Several times throughout the day, stop and ask yourself: "What's one good thing about right now?" It might be as simple as "I'm warm" or "my coffee tastes good" or "my child is healthy."

Look for progress, not just outcomes. Celebrate small improvements, tiny steps forward, moments of healing. "I only cried once today instead of three times" is something to acknowledge.

Notice what you're not missing. Sometimes good is defined by the absence of bad things. "I didn't have an argument today" or "I wasn't walking on eggshells" or "I didn't feel anxious about someone's mood" are all forms of good.

Sometimes you might read this chapter and think, "That's nice for other people, but there really isn't anything good about my situation." If that's where you are, I understand. Some seasons are so difficult that the good is almost invisible.

But I would gently challenge you to look harder. The good might be:

You're still here. You survived something that could have destroyed you. That's not nothing.

You're reading this book. You're actively working on your healing instead of giving up. That's good.

You have people who care about you. Even if it's just one person, even if they're far away, someone cares whether you're okay.

You have basic needs met. You have shelter, food, clothing. These are gifts that millions of people don't have.

You have tomorrow. Your story isn't over. There's still time for things to get better.

You're not the same person you were at your lowest point. Even if progress feels slow, you've grown and changed since your worst day.

If you really can't find anything good about your current situation, that might be a sign that you need additional support. Depression can make it literally impossible to see anything positive. If that's the case, please consider reaching out to a counselor, doctor, or trusted friend.

When you start actively looking for good in your life, something amazing happens: you start finding more of it. This isn't because good things magically start happening - it's because you're training your brain to notice what was already there.

And then, as you notice more good things, you start feeling more hopeful. As you feel more hopeful, you make better decisions. As you make better decisions, more genuinely good things start happening in your life. It becomes a positive spiral instead of a negative one. Plus, when you focus on what's working in your life, you get more energy to invest in making things even better. When you focus only on what's wrong, you feel depleted and discouraged.

I want to be clear about something: finding the good in your life doesn't mean pretending you don't have problems or challenges. It doesn't mean putting on a fake smile and acting like everything is perfect. You can acknowledge that your life is difficult AND that there are good things about it. You can be honest about your struggles AND grateful for your blessings. You can work on improving your situation AND appreciate what's already working. This is both/and thinking, not either/or thinking.

In fact, finding the good in your current situation often gives you the emotional strength and perspective you need to address the problems effectively. When you feel completely overwhelmed by everything that's wrong, it's hard to take positive action. When you can see that some things are working, you feel more capable of fixing the things that aren't.

If you have children, your ability to find good in your current situation is a gift to them too. Children are watching how you handle this difficult time. They're learning from you about resilience, about hope, about how to navigate life's challenges.

When you can genuinely point out good things about your new life - even while acknowledging that it's different and sometimes difficult - you're teaching them that:

- Hard times don't last forever
- There can be silver linings in difficult situations
- It's possible to be grateful even when life isn't perfect
- People can survive and even thrive after major life changes
- There are always reasons to hope

This doesn't mean you have to pretend to be happy all the time or hide your struggles from your children. It means modeling a balanced perspective that includes both the challenges and the blessings of your new reality.

As Christians, finding the good in our circumstances is actually a form of worship. It's trusting that God is still working in our lives even when things don't look the way we wanted them to. It's believing that God can bring good out of painful situations - not that He caused the pain, but that He can redeem it and use it for good purposes.

When we choose gratitude in the middle of difficulty, we're declaring that God's goodness isn't dependent on our circumstances being perfect. We're saying that His love, His faithfulness, His provision are real even when our lives are messy. This kind of gratitude isn't naive or shallow - it's profound and courageous. It takes real faith to thank God for His blessings while you're still in the middle of processing your losses.

You know you're truly thriving in your recovery when finding the good becomes natural instead of forced. When you can genuinely say, "Not everything about my life is horrible" and mean it. When you can see blessings without having to work really hard to find them.

You'll know because:

- You wake up some mornings feeling genuinely grateful for your life
- You can see progress you've made instead of only focusing on how far you have to go
- You feel excited about possibilities instead of just afraid of the future
- You can encourage other people going through similar struggles
- You have energy for things other than just survival
- You can laugh genuinely, not just politely
- You feel curious about life instead of just weary

This doesn't mean every day will be perfect or that you'll never struggle again. It means that hope and gratitude have become part of your regular emotional vocabulary instead of rare visitors.

I promise you there is good in your life right now. I promise you that something positive has come from this difficult experience, even if you can't see it yet. It could be your health - maybe this crisis motivated you to take better care of yourself. It could be your relationships - maybe you've discovered who your real friends are. It could be your strength - maybe you've learned you're more resilient than you ever imagined. It could be your faith - maybe your relationship with God is deeper now than it ever was.

It could be something as simple as the fact that you can sleep peacefully in your own bed, or make decisions without having to negotiate with someone else, or pursue interests that you had to put aside during your marriage. Look for it. Take off those negative glasses and really look for the good in your life right now. I promise you, it's there.

And hey, I think it's great that you're reading this book. You're doing things to help yourself improve. So there's a good thing right there.

Scripture for Finding Good:

"Every good and perfect gift is from above, coming down from the Father of the heavenly lights." - James 1:17

"This is the day the Lord has made; we will rejoice and be glad in it." - Psalm 118:24

"And we know that in all things God works for the good of those who love him." - Romans 8:28

Chapter 15: God HATES Divorce (But He Loves You)

Wrestling with faith and finding peace

"There is now no condemnation for those who are in Christ Jesus." -
Romans 8:1

God hates divorce. He does. The one thing that Jeff and I will never shy away from is the Word of God is the Word of God. What it says is what it says. We don't try to take different verses and apply it to our situation to make us feel better or to make us right. We both had to approach this truth in two different ways.

I've been putting off writing this chapter for months. Not because I don't believe what I'm going to tell you, but because I know how loaded this topic is for Christians going through divorce.I know what it feels like to sit in church and hear sermons about God's design for marriage while your own marriage is crumbling. I know what it feels like to read "God hates divorce" and wonder if that means God hates you. I know what it feels like to question whether you can still be a good Christian if you're getting divorced.

And I know that there are people in the Christian community who will read this chapter and disagree with how I handle this topic. Some will think I'm too soft on divorce. Others will think I'm too hard on divorced people. Some will think I should have more verses and theology. Others will think I should have less.

But I'm not writing this chapter for them. I'm writing it for you - the person who is lying awake at night wondering if God still loves you. The person who is afraid to pray because you think God might be angry with you. The person who is questioning whether there's room in God's family for someone whose marriage didn't make it.

This is for you.

God hates divorce. This is not something we can explain away or soften or reinterpret to make ourselves feel better. It's in Scripture, and it's true. But here's what we need to understand about that statement: God hates divorce because God hates anything that causes His children pain. God hates divorce the same way He hates cancer, car accidents, betrayal, abuse, addiction, and every other thing that brings suffering into our lives.

God doesn't hate divorce because He's arbitrary or legalistic or because He wants to make rules to control us. God hates divorce because He loves us, and He knows that the breaking of marriage covenants causes deep pain to everyone involved - the spouses, the children, the families, the communities.

God hates divorce because divorce represents the shattering of something He designed to be beautiful and permanent. It represents the failure of something He intended to be a picture of His love for us. But - and this is crucial - God's hatred of divorce does not mean God hates divorced people.

You need to understand this: you are not divorce. Divorce is an act, divorce is a certificate, it is a broken covenant . It is not who you are. God loves you. You - not divorced you, not married you, just you. Your identity is not "divorced person." Your identity is "beloved child of God."

God doesn't like a lot of things. God hates car crashes, but car crash victims are not defined by their accidents. God hates sin, but sinners are not beyond His love and redemption. God hates cancer, but cancer patients are not rejected by Him. God hates the things that hurt us, but He never stops loving us.

When God looks at you, He doesn't see "divorced person" first. He sees His child. He sees someone He loves so much that He sent His Son to die for you. He sees someone He has plans for, someone He wants to comfort, someone He wants to use for good purposes.

Jeff and I had to deal with this truth in two different ways, and I want to share both approaches because different people might relate to different responses.

My approach: I felt so much shame and guilt and remorse and just absolutely felt like I had let God down, that I had gotten a divorce even though I had what many would say were biblical grounds for divorce. I still felt like it was a failure and that God hates divorce, so I should feel terrible about it.

For me, this only worked when I went to God and said, "Forgive me, God. Forgive me that I got a divorce. Forgive me, Lord, that I failed at this marriage." And you know what? When He forgives, He loves, and we go forward.

I had to ask God for forgiveness, because I needed to feel clean before Him. I needed to know that my relationship with Him was intact. I needed to hear Him say, "I forgive you, and I love you, and we're going to move forward together."

Jeff's approach: He had biblical grounds for divorce, but he did not feel the need to go and ask God for forgiveness. He said, "This is what the Bible says. I stand on the Word of God, and I take it as a living, breathing word of God. This is what my Lord says, and this is how I'm living my life."

He didn't feel convicted that he needed to ask God for forgiveness for doing something that Scripture permits under certain circumstances. He felt that he was operating within Biblical boundaries and that God understood his situation.

You know, there's two different aspects. Do I think one's right or wrong? No. I think you have to do what within you, within your relationship with God, what He convicts you of. But trust the Holy Spirit on what the Holy Spirit tells you.

This is really important to understand: there's a difference between conviction that comes from the Holy Spirit and condemnation that comes from shame, guilt, or other people's judgment.

Conviction from the Holy Spirit:

- Is specific about actions you need to take or change
- Leads to repentance and restoration
- Comes with hope and a path forward
- Draws you closer to God
- Results in freedom and peace

Condemnation from shame:

- Is vague and makes you feel generally worthless
- Leads to despair and isolation
- Offers no hope or way forward
- Drives you away from God
- Results in bondage and misery

If you feel convicted about specific things you did wrong during your marriage or divorce, that's actually good news. That means God is still working in your life, still wanting to help you grow and change. Respond to that conviction with repentance and trust in God's forgiveness. But if you just feel generally worthless and rejected because you're divorced, that's condemnation, not conviction. That's not from God. God doesn't deal in vague shame and hopelessness.

Some people reading this have what most Christians would consider clear biblical grounds for divorce - adultery, abandonment, abuse. Others are divorced for reasons that feel more complicated or ambiguous.

Here's what I want you to know: your standing with God is not determined by how "justified" your divorce was in other people's eyes. Your relationship with God is between you and God. If you had clear biblical grounds for divorce, you can rest in the knowledge that Scripture provides for your situation.

If your situation was more complicated, you can still bring it to God honestly and trust in His grace. God knows every detail of what you went through. He knows your heart, your efforts, your pain, your impossible choices. Either way, God's love for you is not conditional on having the "right" reasons for divorce.

The shame that many Christians feel about divorce often comes from sources other than God:

Church culture: Some churches, intentionally or not, treat divorce as the unforgivable sin. They make divorced people feel like second-class citizens in God's kingdom.

Other people's opinions: Well-meaning Christians sometimes say hurtful things like "God hates divorce" without any acknowledgment of God's love for divorced people.

Misunderstanding of grace: Some people believe that God's grace covers every other failure but somehow doesn't extend to divorce.

Perfectionism: Some Christians believe they have to get everything right to be worthy of God's love, so any major life failure feels like evidence that God is done with them.

None of these sources of shame are from God. God's voice sounds like love, hope, comfort, and invitation to come closer. If the voice in your head sounds like condemnation, rejection, and hopelessness, that's not God talking.

Do you know what God says about people who are brokenhearted?

"The Lord is close to the brokenhearted and saves those who are crushed in spirit." - Psalm 34:18

That's you. If you're reading this book, you've been brokenhearted. You've been crushed in spirit. And according to Scripture, that doesn't disqualify you from God's presence - it actually draws Him closer to you.

God doesn't stay away from messy, painful situations. He runs toward them. He doesn't avoid broken people. He specializes in healing them.

"He heals the brokenhearted and binds up their wounds." - Psalm 147:3

This is what God does. This is who He is. He's not the God who stands at a distance shaking His head in disappointment. He's the God who gets down in the mess with you and starts putting the pieces back together.

I want to be very clear about this: there is nothing - nothing - that can separate you from God's love. There is no sin so big that God's grace can't cover it. There is no failure so complete that God can't redeem it.

"For I am convinced that neither death nor life, neither angels nor demons, neither the present nor the future, nor any powers, neither height nor depth, nor anything else in all creation, will be able to separate us from the love of God that is in Christ Jesus our Lord." - Romans 8:38-39

Notice what's not on that list? Divorce. Divorce is not powerful enough to separate you from God's love.

You cannot commit murder and be in jail and still have God not have a relationship with you. So don't put that barrier in front of you that God didn't even place there. Don't tell yourself that divorce is somehow worse than every other human failure. Don't give divorce more power over your spiritual life than God does.

One of the biggest lies that shame tells us is that God's good plans for our lives ended when our marriage ended. That somehow we've disqualified ourselves from His blessings, His purposes, His future.

But listen to what God says:

"'For I know the plans I have for you,' declares the Lord, 'plans to prosper you and not to harm you, to give you hope and a future.'" - *Jeremiah 29:11*

Notice that verse doesn't say, "I had plans for you, but you messed them up." It says "I have plans for you" - present tense. God still has plans for your life. Good plans. Plans that include hope and a future.

Your divorce didn't catch God by surprise. It didn't derail His purposes for you. It might have changed what those purposes look like, but it didn't eliminate them. Some of the most powerful ministries, the most beautiful testimonies, the most impactful lives I know have come from people who went through divorce and learned to trust God in a deeper way because of it.

Your story isn't over. In many ways, it might just be beginning.

Here's something that helped me: understanding the difference between God's ideal and God's grace.

God's ideal is that marriages would be permanent, loving, healthy partnerships that reflect His love for us. That's what He designed marriage to be. When that ideal is broken - whether through sin, selfishness, abuse, abandonment, or any other reason - it grieves God's heart.

But God's grace means that when His ideal is broken, He doesn't abandon us. He meets us in our brokenness and helps us build something new. God's ideal was that we would never sin. But when we do sin, His grace covers us. God's ideal was that we would never experience pain, loss, or failure. But when we do, His grace sustains us. Your divorce represents the breaking of God's ideal for marriage. But it doesn't represent the breaking of God's love for you.

So what does this mean for your daily life as a Christian who is divorced?

You can pray without shame. God wants to hear from you. He's not avoiding your prayers or screening your calls. Come to Him with your pain, your questions, your needs, your gratitude.

You can participate fully in church life. You don't have to sit in the back, keep quiet, or assume you're not welcome. You are a full member of God's family.

You can serve others. Your divorce doesn't disqualify you from ministry. In fact, your experience might uniquely qualify you to help others who are struggling.

You can pursue God's calling on your life. Whatever gifts, passions, or purposes God has placed in you, they're still valid. Your marital status doesn't determine your spiritual usefulness.

You can hope for good things in your future. God's blessings aren't reserved for people with perfect track records. His mercies are new every morning for everyone who loves Him.

You can love and be loved again. If God leads you into another relationship, you don't have to carry shame about your past into your future.

If you're still struggling to believe that God loves you as a divorced person, I want to recommend that you look up Mike Winger on YouTube. He has content that goes much deeper into the theological grounds and things that you may be looking for. He'll give you even more resources, and I really want to make this series very simple.

But let me leave you with this: your divorce doesn't define you. It's not the most important thing about you. It's not what God sees first when He looks at you. God sees His beloved child. He sees someone He has plans for. He sees someone He wants to comfort, heal, and use for good purposes.

The biggest thing I could ever tell you is you're not alone, and God is with you.

Grace means that God's love for you is not based on your performance. It's not based on how well you've followed the rules or how successfully you've navigated life's challenges. Grace means that when you fail - and we all fail - God doesn't love you less. When you make mistakes - and we all make mistakes - God doesn't give up on you. When your life doesn't look like what you planned - and whose life ever does? - God doesn't abandon you.

Grace means that God's love for you is steady, unchanging, and unconditional. Your divorce didn't surprise Him, shock Him, or disappoint Him to the point of rejection. God knew every detail of your story before it happened, and He chose to love you anyway. He knew you would go through this difficult experience, and He still had plans to use your life for good.

That's grace. And grace is bigger than divorce. Grace is bigger than failure. Grace is bigger than shame. Grace is big enough to cover you completely.

You've made it through this entire book. You've done the hard work of survival, recovery, and moving toward thriving. You've faced your pain, honored your progress, built your support systems, mourned your losses, worked on forgiveness, let go of what you needed to release, and started dreaming again.

And now you know this: God's love for you is bigger than your divorce. His plans for you didn't end when your marriage ended. His grace is sufficient for every failure, every mistake, every disappointment. You are free to live without shame. You are free to love and be loved. You are free to serve God and others. You are free to hope for good things in your future. You are free to thrive.

God hates divorce because He loves you and hates to see you hurt. But His hatred of your pain doesn't translate to hatred of you. His love for you is steady, unchanging, and eternal. Rest in that love. Build your future on that foundation. Let that truth set you free to live the abundant life God still has planned for you.

You're not alone. God is with you. And you're going to be okay.

Actually, you're going to be more than okay. You're going to thrive.

Scriptures for God's Love:

"The Lord your God is with you, the Mighty Warrior who saves. He will take great delight in you; in his love he will no longer rebuke you, but will rejoice over you with singing." - Zephaniah 3:17

"But God demonstrates his own love for us in this: While we were still sinners, Christ died for us." - Romans 5:8

"Who shall separate us from the love of Christ? Shall trouble or hardship or persecution or famine or nakedness or danger or sword? ...No, in all these things we are more than conquerors through him who loved us." - Romans 8:35, 37

Prayers for Acceptance:

"God, help me believe that Your love for me is not conditional on my marital status. Help me receive Your grace and forgiveness."

"Lord, I'm struggling to believe You still have good plans for my life. Help me trust in Your goodness despite my circumstances."

"Father, show me the difference between conviction that leads to life and condemnation that leads to death. Help me hear Your voice of love."

A Prayer for Freedom:

"Lord God, I come to You honestly about my divorce and the shame I've carried. Help me understand that Your hatred of divorce comes from Your love for me, not Your rejection of me. Help me receive Your grace fully and live in the freedom You've provided through Christ. Show me how to use my experience to glorify You and help others. I choose to believe that Your love for me is bigger than my circumstances and Your plans for me are not over. In Jesus' name, Amen."

Conclusion: The Journey Continues

Your story isn't over - it's just beginning

Scripture for the Road Ahead: *"Being confident of this, that he who began a good work in you will carry it on to completion until the day of Christ Jesus." - Philippians 1:6*

Dear Friend,

If you've made it to this conclusion, you've done something extraordinary. You've walked through some of the hardest chapters any person can face, and you're still here. You're still fighting. You're still believing that there's good ahead.

That's not small. That's heroic.

When Jeff and I first felt called to write this book, we remembered what it felt like to be completely alone in our pain. We remembered searching bookstores and online resources, desperate to find someone who understood what we were going through as Christians facing divorce. We remembered feeling like we were the only believers who had ever walked this road.

We wrote this book because we never want another Christian to feel that alone.

Take a moment to think about where you were when you first picked up this book. Maybe you were in the deepest pit of despair, unable to imagine ever feeling normal again. Maybe you were angry, confused, ashamed, or completely overwhelmed by the enormity of what you were facing.

And now? You've learned that it's okay to hide in God's Word when everything else feels unstable. You've discovered that music can be medicine for your soul. You've given yourself permission to hurt with boundaries. You've learned that being "toxic" for a season is sometimes exactly what healing requires.

You've moved your body to heal your heart. You've found your place in the body of Christ, even when it looked different than before. You've embraced a new reality you never wanted but have learned to navigate with grace.

You've honored yourself for surviving something that could have destroyed you. You've helped others help you by being honest about your needs. You've done the hard work of mourning what you've lost. You've worked on forgiveness - both giving it and receiving it.

You've let go of reminders while honoring your past. You've started dreaming again, believing that your future can be beautiful even if it looks different than you planned. You've found good in your present circumstances. And you've wrestled with the truth that God hates divorce but loves you completely.

That's an incredible journey. You should be proud of how far you've come.

Through these pages, we hope you've discovered some truths that will carry you forward:

You are not alone. There are Christians who have walked this path before you, who understand your pain, and who are cheering you on from the other side of recovery. More importantly, God is with you in every step of this journey.

Your worth is not determined by your marital status. You are beloved by God not because you're married or single, but because you're His child. Your identity is rooted in something much deeper and more permanent than your relationship status.

Healing is possible. Not just surviving - thriving. Not just getting through each day, but actually building a life you love. It might look different than you originally planned, but different doesn't mean less than.

Your story isn't over. Divorce feels like an ending, and in many ways it is. But it's also a beginning. The chapters you write from here forward can be filled with purpose, joy, love, and hope.

God's grace is bigger than your circumstances. There is nothing you've done, no mistake you've made, no failure you've experienced that puts you outside the reach of God's love and redemption.

Your recovery doesn't end with the last page of this book. Healing is a lifelong journey, not a destination you arrive at and never have to think about again.

There will be setbacks. There will be days when you feel like you're back at square one. There will be triggers you didn't expect, grief that resurfaces at unexpected moments, and new challenges you haven't faced before.

That's normal. That's part of the process. Don't let temporary setbacks convince you that you're not making progress or that you're somehow failing at recovery.

Keep doing the work. Keep finding your hiding places in God's Word. Keep moving your body when your heart feels heavy. Keep honoring yourself for the progress you've made. Keep looking for the good in your circumstances. Keep believing that God has beautiful plans for your future.

Keep growing. The tools you've learned in this book aren't just for getting through divorce - they're life skills that will serve you well in whatever comes next. The resilience you've developed, the self-awareness you've gained, the relationship with God you've deepened - these are gifts that will bless you for the rest of your life.

Keep helping others. One of the most beautiful things about healing is that it qualifies you to help others who are still in the pit you've climbed out of. Your experience, your story, your survival - these are gifts you can offer to others who are walking the road you've traveled.

We've talked a lot about thriving in this book, and we want to be clear about what we mean. Thriving doesn't mean your life is perfect. It doesn't mean you never have bad days or difficult moments. It doesn't mean you've forgotten your past or that you never feel sad about what you've lost.

Thriving means you've learned to build a beautiful life with the pieces you have. It means you wake up most mornings with hope instead of dread. It means you can see God's goodness even in circumstances you wouldn't have chosen. It means you believe your best days are ahead of you, not behind you.

Thriving means you've stopped just surviving and started really living.

And we believe - no, we know - that's possible for you. We've seen it in our own lives. We've seen it in the lives of countless others who have walked this path. God specializes in bringing beauty from ashes, in making all things new, in writing stories of redemption.

Your story of redemption is still being written.

As we close this book, we want to pray over you:

Heavenly Father, we lift up every person who has walked through these pages with us. We thank You for their courage to keep going when giving up felt easier. We thank You for their willingness to do the hard work of healing.

Lord, we pray that You would continue the good work You've started in them. Help them to see themselves through Your eyes - beloved, chosen, valuable, and full of potential. Help them to trust Your plans for their future even when they can't see the whole picture.

Give them strength for the journey ahead. Surround them with people who will love them well and support their continued healing. Open doors of opportunity, relationship, and purpose that they can't even imagine right now.

Help them to be patient with themselves as they continue to grow. Remind them on hard days that setbacks are not failures, that healing isn't linear, and that You are still working all things together for their good.

Use their stories, their pain, their healing, and their hope to bring comfort to others who are walking this same difficult road. Let them be living proof that people can not just survive divorce, but thrive after it.

And Lord, we pray that years from now, when they look back on this season of their lives, they'll be able to see Your faithfulness woven through every chapter - even the ones that felt hopeless at the time.

In Jesus' name, Amen.

Jeff and I want you to know that writing this book has been one of the most meaningful projects of our lives. Knowing that these words might help even one person feel less alone in their pain, more hopeful about their future, and more confident in God's love has made every difficult memory worth revisiting.

We believe God brought you to this book because He wanted you to know you're not alone. We believe He used our stories to speak hope into your story. And we believe He's going to use your story to bring hope to others.

You are not the same person who started reading this book. You're stronger, braver, more resilient, and more aware of your own worth. You've survived something that could have destroyed you, and you're still here, still fighting, still believing. That's extraordinary.

Keep going, dear friend. Keep healing. Keep growing. Keep believing. Keep hoping. Your story isn't over. In fact, we have a feeling the best chapters are still to come.

With love and hope for your beautiful future,

Teresa and Jeff McKelvey

"'For I know the plans I have for you,' declares the Lord, 'plans to prosper you and not to harm you, to give you hope and a future.'" - Jeremiah 29:11

Additional Resources for Your Journey

Tools, support, and continued growth opportunities

Essential Support Resources

DivorceCare

Website: www.divorcecare.org
What it offers: Faith-based divorce recovery support groups available in churches nationwide. Includes weekly meetings, video sessions, and workbooks specifically designed for Christians going through divorce.

Why we recommend it: This was the first resource Teresa found that made her feel less alone. The combination of biblical teaching and practical support is invaluable during early recovery.

To find a group: Use the group finder on their website or call local churches to ask if they offer DivorceCare programs.

Crisis Support

National Suicide Prevention Lifeline: 988
Crisis Text Line: Text HOME to 741741
National Domestic Violence Hotline: 1-800-799-7233

If you're having thoughts of hurting yourself or others, please reach out immediately. Your life matters, and help is available.

Music for Healing

Jason Gray - "Love Will Have the Final Word"

Available on: Spotify, Apple Music, Amazon Music, YouTube
Standout songs:

- "Not Right Now" (for when everyone keeps saying "it'll be okay")
- "When I Say Yes" (about surrender and trust)
- "Love Will Have the Final Word" (hope for the future)

Why this album matters: This album speaks directly to the pain of divorce while offering hope. Jason Gray wrote many of these songs during his own divorce journey.

Other Recommended Artists for Healing:

- **Lauren Daigle** - "You Say," "Rescue"
- **Kari Jobe** - "I Am Not Alone," "Healer"
- **Hillsong United** - "Oceans," "So Will I"
- **Chris Tomlin** - "Good Good Father," "Is He Worthy"

Deeper Biblical Study

Mike Winger - YouTube Channel

Channel: @MikeWinger
 Recommended playlists:

- "Divorce and Remarriage" series (comprehensive biblical analysis)
- "Biblical Manhood and Womanhood" (understanding identity after divorce)

Why we recommend: Mike provides thorough, biblically sound teaching on complex topics related to divorce, remarriage, and Christian living. His approach is gracious while being theologically rigorous.

Bible Study Resources

YouVersion Bible App
 Download: Free on all platforms
 Includes dozens of divorce recovery and healing reading plans.

Books for Continued Growth

For General Divorce Recovery:

- **"Boundaries" by Henry Cloud and John Townsend** - Essential for learning healthy relationships
- **"The Life Recovery Bible" (NLT)** - Bible with notes specifically for healing and recovery
- **"Rising Strong" by Brené Brown** - About getting back up after failure and disappointment

For Understanding God's Heart:

- **"The Ragamuffin Gospel" by Brennan Manning** - About God's grace for imperfect people
- **"Jesus Calling" by Sarah Young** - Daily devotional focusing on God's love and presence

---

Practical Life Support

Financial Assistance:

211 - Dial 2-1-1 for local resources including food banks, utility assistance, and emergency funds
Feeding America - www.feedingamerica.org - Food bank locator
Salvation Army - Local assistance with utilities, rent, and basic needs

Legal Aid:

Legal Aid Society - Free or low-cost legal assistance for low-income individuals
State Bar Association - Most states offer lawyer referral services and limited free consultations

Professional Counseling:

Psychology Today - www.psychologytoday.com - Therapist finder with filters for Christian counselors, divorce specialists, and insurance accepted
Focus on the Family - 1-855-771-4357 - Free counseling consultation and referrals
American Association of Christian Counselors - www.aacc.net - Directory of Christian counselors

---

Online Communities and Support

Divorce Support Groups:

DivorcedGirl Smiling - www.divorcedgirlsmiling.com - Blog and community for divorced women
Single Mom's Circle - Facebook group with Christian focus
Life After Divorce - Various Facebook groups (search for Christian-focused ones)

General Christian Support:

She Reads Truth Community - Online Bible study community
Proverbs 31 Ministries - www.proverbs31.org - Encouragement for Christian women
FamilyLife - www.familylife.com - Resources for all family situations including single parents

---

Apps for Daily Support

Prayer and Meditation:

- **Abide** - Christian meditation and sleep stories
- **Pray.com** - Prayer requests, daily prayers, and community
- **First 5** - 5-minute daily Bible study from Proverbs 31 Ministries

General Wellness:

- **Headspace** - Meditation and mindfulness (has specific programs for dealing with grief)
- **Calm** - Sleep stories, meditation, relaxation
- **MyFitnessPal** - Nutrition tracking when you're learning to cook for one

---

Emergency Planning

If You're in Immediate Danger:

- **Call 911**
- **National Domestic Violence Hotline: 1-800-799-7233**
- **Text LOVEIS to 22522**

Safety Planning Resources:

The Hotline.org - Safety planning tools and resources
WomensLaw.org - Legal information for abuse survivors
National Coalition Against Domestic Violence - www.ncadv.org

Resources for Children

Books to Help Kids Process Divorce:

- **"Dinosaurs Divorce" by Laurene Krasny Brown** (ages 3-8)
- **"It's Not Your Fault, KoKo Bear" by Vicki Lansky** (ages 3-8)
- **"Two Homes" by Claire Masurel** (ages 4-8)
- **"Standing on My Own Two Feet" by Tamara Schmitz** (teens)

Professional Help for Children:

Play Therapy International - www.a4pt.org - Find play therapists for children
American Professional Society on the Abuse of Children - www.apsac.org - Resources for children who have experienced trauma

---

Long-term Growth Resources

If You're Ready to Consider Dating Again:

"Boundaries in Dating" by Henry Cloud and John Townsend
"How to Get a Date Worth Keeping" by Henry Cloud

If You're Considering Remarriage:

"Smart Stepfamilies" by Ron Deal
"The Smart Stepfamily Marriage" by Ron Deal and David H. Olson

For Personal Development:

"Daring Greatly" by Brené Brown - About vulnerability and courage

---

How to Find Local Resources

1. **Call 211** - This connects you to local resources for almost any need
2. **Contact local churches** - Even if you don't attend, many churches have assistance programs
3. **Check your county's website** - Look for "human services" or "social services" departments
4. **Ask your doctor** - Medical professionals often know local mental health and support resources
5. **Contact local libraries** - Librarians are excellent at finding resources and many libraries host support groups

---

Creating Your Own Support Network

Questions to Ask When Seeking Help:

- Do you have experience working with divorced Christians?
- What is your approach to faith and healing?
- Do you offer payment plans or sliding scale fees?
- How do you handle confidentiality?
- What should I expect from our first session?

Red Flags to Avoid:

- Anyone who immediately tells you that you should have stayed married
- Counselors who push their personal beliefs about divorce instead of helping you heal
- Support groups that feel more like gossip sessions than healing environments
- Anyone who makes you feel ashamed for your divorce

A Final Word About Resources

Remember, not every resource will be right for every person. What helps one person might not help another, and that's okay. Give yourself permission to try different things and stick with what works for you.

Also remember that using resources isn't a sign of weakness - it's a sign of wisdom. Getting help shows that you're committed to your healing and growth.

You don't have to use all of these resources. Start with one or two that feel most relevant to your current needs. As you grow and change, your needs may change too, and you can explore different resources.

The most important thing is that you don't try to do this alone. God has provided many ways for His people to support each other through difficult times. Let yourself be supported.

You've got this, and you're not alone.

www.ingramcontent.com/pod-product-compliance
Lightning Source LLC
Chambersburg PA
CBHW070936130626
46555CB00001B/462